DOUBT~LESS

DO MORE

TRUDY SIMMONS

CONTENTS

Dedication   v
Acknowledgements   vii
Introduction   ix

1. How to doubt yourself and get in your own way …   1
2. How to fail forward … fast   8
3. How to make the next decision   16
4. How to take a comfortable risk   23
5. Find the people who fuel your fire   31
6. How to overcome the little voices of doubt   39
7. Learn how to trust yourself   45
8. How to build self-belief   51
9. How to build your confidence   57
10. How to ask for help   65
11. How to let go and move on   76
12. Why taking personal responsibility helps our mindset   83
13. Creating clarity   88
14. Deciding on direction   95
15. Finding focus   103
16. Becoming accountable   110
17. The knowing and the growing   117
18. How to be more "Doubt~less"   123
     Epilogue   128

About Trudy Simmons   131
About The Daisy Chain Group   133
You want more?   135

Printed in the United Kingdom
First Printing, 2024

Cover design by: Gemma Storey from Infinity Creative
Photography by: Amanda Clarke Photography

ISBN: 9781739743123 (paperback)
ISBN: 9781739743130 (eBook)

The Daisy Chain Group International Ltd
Hampshire, UK

connect@thedaisychaingroup.com

DEDICATION

For Jody and Jean

The wise and the wondrous: my precious little sister and my
heartfelt Grandma.
Both left, but never gone; always felt and not forgotten.

As Grandma would say in every birthday card, "TLC"

Tender Loving Care to us all.

ACKNOWLEDGEMENTS

Allow me to be long and indulgent in my acknowledgements of the wonderful people that have helped me get to this stage of the book. I love reading acknowledgements in other people's books and always worry that they are worrying that they have forgotten someone, or that someone reads it and thinks, "Why not me?". So, to those that are not mentioned, you are appreciated; these are the people that I need to mention at this part of the journey.

My Grandma, Jean May Francis Simmons, left me four days after I got married; in her time here, there was never a conversation that she didn't tell me "You can do anything", that " You are a hard worker" and that "Laughter is the best medicine"; all of this you will find in this book. I am 'my Grandmother's Granddaughter' and very proud of that. Thank you for your 96 years Grandma; I knew you, loved you and listened to you for half your life, the whole of my life. I'll miss our little chats and holding your hand for comfort. I know you would be telling everyone about this book - and I bet you are telling everyone who will listen wherever you are now.

To Gillian Jones-Williams, thank you for changing my life, helping me with my confidence in the things that matter, guiding me with your innate way of encouragement which has taken me out of my comfort zone in all areas of my life. For not allowing me to run, hide, or give up. For your wisdom in enabling me to emerge, rise and be myself – in all ways. I appreciate it all.

To my newly initiated mother-in-law, Chris Wayman, your gentle nudges came at times that I thought I would falter, thank you for them. Thank you for being a patient Editor-in-Chief, a master of the English language, and for your willingness to let some "Trudy-isms" slip through the dictionary in your head. I'm so grateful for your persistence in this, the first of many endeavours together. I know how proud you are of me and that means so much.

To my long-suffering - SCRATCH THAT - to my very lucky, newly-happy-husband, Richard, I waited a long time to find you, you're welcome …

This year has been the best so far, and many more to come.

INTRODUCTION

When I was born, I didn't doubt myself … and I DOUBT that you did either. So what on earth happens between then and now that makes us have all the fears, all the doubts, all the conversations with ourselves? (I hope it isn't just me that does that – FULL ON conversations answering and questioning, all in my head!).

This book came about because I was talking to a business coaching client and hearing her explanations (and excuses) about why she wasn't putting herself out there, why she was staying in her comfort zone, why it was easier to play small, why it was too hard, too much, too icky, too salesy, too visible … all the things that we put in our way, and I realised that all of those things were in me too, and probably in most businesswomen.

I wondered how do we feel the doubts, know the doubts, see the doubts of others and yet do it anyway? When we are feeling "It's all too much", and are unsure about our level of success, what are the differences, the steps, the formulas (although I doubt there is a 'one formula fits all') or the processes that can help us all to doubt ourselves LESS? How can we grow in confidence – begone the self-sabotage – and how can we stare down the imposter syndrome and cry out, "I CAN DO THIS" at the top of our lungs and then feel the surge of strength, resilience and grit to be able to dig deeper and do something differently?

On the front of this book you will see a part of the Doubt~less logo family. This is really important to me. My business is called The Daisy Chain Group because daisies make me happy, they look for the sunshine and they blossom. For this logo my very clever brand designer Gemma Storey from Infinity Creative added in the three stages of a daisy, which are very significant to how we approach things. Each and every night the daisy closes up its petals to protect itself and rest for the night. That symbolises how we feel when we are doubting ourselves – our petals/minds are closed, we are protecting ourselves from the possibilities. Then we have the half open daisy, that bit in-between sleeping and waking, where all ideas are possible and anything can happen, so we instinctively start to open our minds. The final stage is where we are doubting ourselves less and the daisy opens to look up at the opportunities, the possibilities and the sun to shine down on it, so that it can soak it all up and do it all again the next day. This representation is under my name on the front cover.

You have picked up this book because you know you are meant for more, you want to have an impact, leave a legacy, influence and empower people with whatever you do in your business. At the end of each chapter are a few "Things to do differently" – if you do these things/tasks/suggestions/ideas, and build up with each chapter, ANYTHING is possible.

Change doesn't happen overnight, it happens in each little step you are willing to take for yourself. So make little changes, take the baby steps and move forward with less~Doubt.

HOW TO DOUBT YOURSELF AND GET IN YOUR OWN WAY ...

A PERSONAL TALE ...

Yes, you read that chapter title correctly. Sometimes, we need to look at where and how and WHY we doubt ourselves, where it shows up the most, how it affects what we are able to do and why we let it.

We all have a story, a journey, a path that has led us to where we are now. Some are the sorrowful tales of woe and some are the accounts of triumph and 'Rocky' fist-pumping resilience.

At times, we may have fallen into the victim mentality and at others we will have found our survivor strength; but at ALL TIMES, we can change our minds and make better/different decisions ... believe me, I have learned all of this the hard way.

I was walking up a mountain with a friend once, and I decided to walk on a teeny-tiny path above hers. She looked at me and said, "Trudy, why do you always find the harder path to take?" – so very deep, and a question for us all to answer.

MY CORPORATE CAREER

Firstly, let me tell you, I spent the first 25 years of my career in a corporate job of one kind or another. And, in my last stint as an employable person, I found myself burnt out, confidence killed and a bumbling wreck, chewed up and spat out of a company that I felt I gave everything to, and then ... it was no longer. I felt useless. All my fears came crashing down around me and I thought that I had nowhere to go, I was stuck, without a direction and with no help or support ... at least, that is how it felt to me at the time.

I had spent my whole life telling people (and myself) that I would always work for someone else, because I am so much better at putting everything in for other people. I need to be needed, I like to be helpful, I can be of service.

I ended up having reached some heady heights of the ladder with a lot of bravado, without much confidence, and having no tools to deal with the scrapes along the way.

On the flip side of "I'll be better at working for someone else" was "I can't work for myself because I won't care enough about the outcome" – what I came to realise was that this was just a protection mechanism for any and all failures along the way in my business – that snarky voice that says "See ... I told you that you couldn't work for yourself!". Ohhh, I can just see the scrunched up face of derision, with the ever-so-helpful eye roll and the flounce of the head turn.

Coming out of my corporate career and finding myself unemployed was terrifying and, with a hefty mortgage to pay on my dream home in Melbourne, I was scared all the time. I realise now that it was that scared and fearful feeling which kept me stuck for quite some time. I saw that emotions can cloud our decisions; they make us doubt our decisions even when we feel as though we are doing our best. It taught me the lessons of who I really am, not who I had been to get to this point, but who I really am now.

I had to unlearn all that I had learned to get me here. The tough exterior, the no-nonsense attitude, the balls-to-the-wall get it done approach that I had, which was often detrimental to my health. I took some time, in counselling (hello 10 years of counselling!), in meditation, in walking really long distances, in letting go of the anger and hurt. Eventually my adorable little heart cracked open enough to be able to play, feel and have fun again, and slowly I became ME.

TRUDY AS A TODDLER

Back to the beginning, I was born a baby (KIDDING) ... I was the most adorable baby and toddler, I looked like tiny tears (the doll!), with little tight blonde curls and a button nose.

I remember doubting things as a child, even as a toddler; but the memories that stick in my head are of overcoming the obstacles, creating the systems for charging forward, learning my patterns of destruction and then watching them pan out. Hindsight is a wonderful thing and, being able to look back now, (I have half a century to look back over ... I know ... I don't look that old!) I can see the patterns.

As a child, my Dad would test our resolve. I have three sisters and two brothers, but when I was little, it was just me and my one little sister for a period of time. My Dad would connect ropes between trees and make us (help us!) walk the tightrope holding onto a rope above our heads. Now ... one thing that you need to know about me, is that I am "somewhat" dramatic ... I have a wonderful way (my words!) of dramatising any and all situations. It makes my world very colourful and I'm sticking to that story! This memory of the tears and tantrums to walk a 15 foot length of rope about three feet off the ground (I SWEAR it felt like 15 feet off the ground) is a tale of overcoming doubt.

What was the worst that could happen? I could fall... Dad would catch me. I could hurt my little hands on the rope ... then again ... I might not. OR, I could just put one foot in front of the other, with tears in my eyes, a little screech with each tiny footstep, a whimper with every hand movement and get to the end of the rope. I remember, that way that children do, looking at my Dad, who was looking up at me, and part of me was hoping that he would "save me", take me down off the ropes and let me run around on the grass; part of me was looking at him to see if there was sympathy, empathy, something that would tell me that he knew my pain (dramatic!), but all I saw was the eyes of someone saying "You can do it, get it done"; that isn't a bad thing, it didn't give me an option for giving up. And sometimes, we don't want that option, but if it is given, we take it. He was firm in his "You can do this, get it done" face. Boo hiss boo.

I can see now that that look was one of reassurance and encouragement, but it doesn't feel like it when you are in the midst of what is going on in your own head.

So I would walk that rope, I would get it done; then I would jump down, turn to Dad and ask to do it again … and again … and again … until my confidence grew.

And it did.

MY BUSINESS

That is what I do for people now, it is what has grown my business across continents. I have a face of reassurance and encouragement, but a voice that says "You can do it" and then "Get it done"! I am all about accountability, with clear direction and focus on what you want to get done. I have an approach of "This is already done, don't get in your own way to get there". Sometimes, we all need that gentle nudge of being on the tightrope, looking down for a way out, and seeing that we just needed the support to get to the end of that rope, that task, that project, that level of visibility.

THIS BOOK

When I started writing this book, I honestly thought that I was writing it for "other people" who doubt themselves, because I don't doubt myself. Pahhh – hilarious Trudy, take a look in the proverbial mirror. I have found myself riddled with doubt writing this book ... who will read it (please let me know if you do!), and do other people feel like I do? Am I making myself too visible? What will people say about it? How will it be received? Is this even worth it? What if my family read it? I let all these things get in my head and, as the thoughts all took hold, I stopped ... I stopped writing, I stopped thinking, I stopped being able to get the words out of me and onto paper. But in doing that, I felt so sick and confused, because I knew in my heart that I needed and wanted to do this.

Then, as the strength of thoughts returned, and my posse of people encouraged me, I did it. I saw the potential in getting this out there and it is very important to me to always do what I say I'm going to do. In seeing the people that care about me, telling me to do what I felt was right, I had an almighty heart-bursting DO IT feeling and I got out of my own way and started with that one word that had started all of this ... how can I doubt myself LESS? When I feel like this, I talk to my sister Jody and my wonderful Grandma and ask them if I'm doing the right thing. The answer, invariably, is a giggle and a YES!

MY SISTER

I have a clear memory of when my sister Jody was born when I was six years old. I remember so many visits to the hospital for what felt like months to see her, as the doctors slowly worked their way from, "We are sorry, but we believe that Jody is deaf, mute and blind", with the fears of my parents running through my body and the tears on their faces, trying not to affect me and my little sister Carly. All I could see was another little sister, a baby who needed her big sister. We got dressed up in the scrubs to go to the incubator and stand on a chair to look through the window of the door to see her. I remember my Mum saying "She is watching the mobile go around above her incubator" and I KNEW she could hear us.

Jody had severe cerebral palsy and, through that gift, it made me see the potential in everyone more.

Jody, in her 33 years here, never doubted me, never doubted my commitment to her and we had a bond that was, and is, unbreakable. At each twist and turn of her life, my family would find clever ways to adapt and fix environments to better assist her. We are all very capable people, and I think that this comes from being brought up without a level of doubt that others may have. I remember someone saying to me when I was young "Jody must be such a burden on your family – no offence" – well … firstly OFFENCE TAKEN and secondly, it wasn't how we looked at the situation. That is not to say that things were easy, but again, with hindsight, I never doubted that I got what I needed from her and she got what she needed from me. On the saddest of days when she died (24th December 2013), I Skyped her from Australia to her hospital bed and told her to go to sleep if she needed to. I said, "I know who you are to me and you know who I am to you, I don't need to be there Jode, I love you, go to sleep now".

Losing Jody was one of the biggest turning points of my life, but that is for another chapter. What it showed me is that there are levels of the danged onion that need peeling to see the next layer of doubt and fear that needs to be acknowledged. But the lessons that I learned from having her and loving her so deeply will stay with me forever.

So many people, close friends, family, professionals, doubted Jody. They doubted that the person inside her was happy – because how could she be "like that"? Well, let me tell you, that woman took all the doubt around her, spun it around, turned her face purple with rage and then blew it out and laughed like you have never seen a person laugh. Her lips would turn blue from laughing so hard – I miss that so much. She and I had the same approach to the world around us. Trust everyone, until they let you down. Laugh, laugh, laugh, be cheeky and have fun. Like when I would say to her "Do you want to go out for a walk?" and she would say "I can't …" and as I turned to her, she was laughing that laugh of hers, to her own joke – I do that too, I can crack myself up!

LET'S CRACK ON!

And so in my sorrowful tales of woe and accounts of triumph and Rocky-fist-pumping resilience, I have learned to let the doubters fuel me, to take on board all that has got me here, all the things that I have let get in my way and the lessons I have taken on board.

Doubters gonna doubt (what an awful phrase!), but you can make the decision to do something differently from NOW ... so let's read this together and take the steps towards your potential.

THINGS TO DO DIFFERENTLY:

1. Unlearn what you need to in order to become YOU
2. Look for the reassurance that you need to get it done.
3. You have massive potential – what is it?

HOW TO FAIL FORWARD ... FAST

In our lives, we want so much to be successful and, in that wanting, we give so much power to failure. We can get so scared of putting ourselves out there that we create all the stoppers and obstacles that we need to overcome before we have even started.

We start with this wonderful vision of what we want to be, or what we want to build. We picture what that will look like, how we will feel, and then somehow, the fears and failures creep in, like a person with a sledgehammer who is bashing at our walls of structure, and we allow those thoughts to be and feel bigger than the success we are aiming for. And this isn't just in business ... it's in life.

So let's start with the what-if's.

What if we fail

What if we can't do it

What if it isn't possible

What if the trolls come out

What if someone we love says something that hurts our confidence

What if they don't buy from us

What if they don't like us

What if they don't want what we offer

What if they tear us down

What if they don't understand why we are working so hard

What if they don't support us

And so the list goes on...

Ahhhh, yes... but then...

What if we did the work

What if we succeeded

What if we grew the audience

What if we put the time in

What if we got real clarity on what it is we want

What if we planned for the success

What if we could see it clearly

What if we didn't let anything get in our way

What if we didn't let anyone get in our way

What if we just listened to ourselves and the positives

What if we believed in ourselves

Firstly ... Who are "they"???? It might be that you need to make a list of who "they" are and protect yourself from sharing too much with them until it is done.

I have had my business for over 14 years and one of things that I have learned is not to put too much stock in "them", especially if they don't have their own business and, more importantly, if they are not your audience, your ideal customer, your people. What we learn is that everyone has an opinion and, sometimes, those opinions come from their own fears of failing. They think that they are protecting you by stopping you in your tracks, but this is your life, your business, your time, so how much do you believe in what you are doing?

Failing forward is a powerful concept because we learn from failures. If you are just willing to fail and give up, then you aren't learning from what happened and doing something differently.

I couldn't count the number of times that I have had failures in my business. Some have been monumental. Some have been financial. Some have been emotional. But all have been massive learnings and I know that each time it has happened, I have grown or changed in some way that was necessary for the future.

LOOK BACK TO LEAP FORWARD

Have you been in a situation and thought that you never want to think about that again? Have you finished a project, a service, a product, put it out there, to tumbleweed and then shelved it and moved on? I have … lots of times, sometimes with over a year of hard slog, sweat, tears and drama and then cancelled it almost immediately, for various reasons and usually because my heart is no longer in it. One was a massive online course that I created with someone else; over 60 classes; that is 60 videos, 60 scripts, 60 worksheets, 60 powerpoint presentations; an immense amount of work in the planning, the launching, the audience, the social media, the marketing and then we shelved it within six months of launching it. It was a hard thing to do, but it was the right thing to do at the time, for me.

The first thing that I do is reflect. How did I get here?

Lots of people suggest journalling at this point and I love the idea of this, but it doesn't suit how I do things. Looking back over the term of the endeavour can give you many an insight into how to do things differently in the future. If you like writing then journal it out, if you like talking then find the right person/people to share exactly what has happened. There is a way of doing the reflection that will suit you – TRY them all and see what feels best. Sometimes I write it in brief on a piece of paper and burn it (after I have put it on the floor and stamped on it repeatedly), which is very satisfying!

Start with how you feel now, get it all out.

Move on to the specifics of where or how it got to this – be honest with yourself, it is easy to think "they didn't buy from me" – but did you do enough to get it out there in the first place, or what could you do more of in the future?

A few years ago, I managed to get myself into an awful situation in a partnership in a business venture. I knew at the beginning that it felt wrong to me, but I let it go too far and it ended up completely debilitating my business and my health. I left broken; my confidence in total tatters; my belief systems in pieces around me; my mind searching for the good and not finding anything to grasp onto. It was one of the pivotal moments in my life and business because I had to start again, but before I could do that, I had to look long and hard at how I had got to this place; I had to reflect HARD.

I could see how it had happened and my part in it, but that just made me feel sick, stupid and naïve. And feeling those feelings didn't help me to move forward and I needed to fail forward and let the failure go ... fast. I have always supported myself financially through my business (and my career), so I didn't have the time to sit and wallow and do all the "woe is me" dramatics, I needed to decide what was next. But it wasn't that easy, my mind was a scrambled-topsy-turvy mess, my mental state was questionable, I was malfunctioning – I had a system error that was flashing on the blue screen – you get it!

After my reflections, I had to change my MIND.

CHANGING YOUR MIND

I am a perpetually positive person; I live in my brightly coloured world where everything and everyone is positive. And when something as big as a failure happens, I lose my sense of direction and my ability to see the world through my rosy-pink-tinted-glasses. So, I needed to figure out how to get back to that, whilst also looking after myself, repairing and rejuvenating my broken pieces and building an income in my business ... again.

So I sat my sweet-self down and gave myself a jolly good talking to. I heard the words that I was saying and using (mostly in my head!) and made a conscious decision to change them. I needed to change how I was thinking, I needed to change my mindset, I needed to be able to say all the good things, so that how I felt could catch up with what I was saying and what I was thinking.

TRY IT! If you are sitting there saying things like "Why isn't this happening?", "When will I be successful?", "Why is this so hard?" – change it to the positive and say it until it makes sense ... NOTE: this may take time, but it is better than staying stuck!

Have you heard of a Growth Mindset? I read about it in a book called *Mindset* by Dr Carol Dweck and I realised that that was what I needed to adopt to be able to do more. It really is about looking around you and deciding to be persistent, despite everything. It is looking at failure and obstacles as opportunities to do things differently next time.

And then comes the plan ...

PLANNING FOR THE FUTURE

You are brilliant – 'nuff said!

From that feeling of failure, the sometimes devastating defeat that can come with that, the debilitating fear of making the same mistakes again, the trepidation of dipping your tippy-toe back in the water, to the LET'S DO THIS feeling of ... that was then, this is now, no more doubt (or at least LESS doubt than there was), dip your toe back in the water, it is warm and welcoming and you are ready ... so let's plan for the future.

The length of time that that can all take is dependent on YOU. This particular failure of mine took about two months to get over and through and move forward – not without its daily/weekly wibble-wobbles of worries and doubts, but still ... onwards I went!

And so we plan ... how do you plan best? I love to do it on big sheets of paper to begin with, with coloured pens for each income stream, funnel and process. Then each of those is broken down into the time that each service will need on a weekly/monthly basis. When I can see it, I can create it. And when I can create it, I get excited, and when I get excited, my confidence grows and when my confidence grows, my sense of past failures pales into the past.

It makes it very hard to bring doubt in when there is a plan in place for the success. It doesn't mean that there are no doubts, but it does make it easier to see the future. When you can see and feel the future, you can fail forward fast!

Sounds too simple? Try it and let me know how it works for you. Sometimes, simplicity is the way, but we try to overcomplicate things to justify the reasons why something doesn't get done. Re-read that sentence and think ruh-roh, I see it now!

And finally in your fail forward formula...

CELEBRATE!

I have no doubt that we will be talking about celebrating a lot through this book. Why? Because we don't do it enough. We forget to celebrate the big things, let alone the little things along the way. Celebrating failure might seem counterintuitive, but bear with me here.

When you are at school and you learn something, or you are tested, you get a gold star, or a "Well done" from the teacher. Now YOU are the student and the teacher, so you need to give yourself a "Well done" for the lessons that you have learned along the way. Many of those lessons are hard, some can be life changing, they may be hard fought and test your resilience, but here you are. Learning, reflecting and planning.

So how are you going to celebrate your-fine-self? It is an individual thing when you think about celebrating, but here are some ideas:

Eat a whole chocolate cake

Go for a walk

Spa day

Sit and read in a café for a couple of hours

Go out for lunch with friends

Go out for lunch by yourself!

Whatever you do – acknowledge what it has taken to get to this point. As I said, you are BRILLIANT, so shine bright.

What would help you to feel celebrated? A lot of the businesswomen who I work with work by themselves, so celebrating can feel selfish, or comes with a sense of guilt, of taking the time and money to do something for themselves … and to that, I say tish-tosh, pish-posh, codswallop!

If you are not willing to invest in celebrating all that you do on a daily basis, then how are you going to be able to realise how quickly you overcame the things that you put in your way. Think back over the last week and name the things that you thought you couldn't do and you did them anyway. Think of the little things that you may have felt you failed at and yet, here you are. Think of the daily juggle of being all the things to all the people AND have your own business – you are SPECTACULAR, so praise yourself.

Buy yourself that book that you want, invest in that fancy-pants notebook that seems extravagant, go out for that coffee or lunch and take time out from sitting at your desk staring at a screen. Book onto that silent retreat (if that is your thing ... each to their own ...).

Please remember to celebrate yourself, your wins, your learnings, your failings and the fact that you are still here, doing what you do, for the audience that listens to you, buys from you and waits to hear from you.

If you fail, fail fast, fail forward and celebrate the ka-ka out of it!

THINGS TO DO DIFFERENTLY:

1. Reflect and journal, plan, analyse.
2. Change your MIND
3. Plan for the future
4. Celebrate the past

HOW TO MAKE THE NEXT DECISION

There is a podcast for this book, called ... wait for it ... Doubt~less. I have interviewed some really fascinating, driven and inspirational women who have very different careers and through these careers have had to overcome some huge doubts, both of their own making and from others around them. One of the threads that I have seen and heard in these interviews (and from my own life) is that we make quick decisions about how to move forward.

That isn't to say that the decisions are ill-thought-out or reckless; they are considered decisions about the pros and cons, but a lot of times those pros and cons are, "Do I want to stay feeling/doing this?", or "Do I want to do/be something different?".

But how do we make these decisions and why is it important to be able to see them, make them and action them?

RECOGNISE THAT CHANGE IS NEEDED

First we need to be able to recognise that there is a change that needs to be made. Sometimes this is the hardest bit of the equation because, if we recognise it, bring attention to it, have conscious thoughts around it, then we may have to do something about it.

And when decision making is not your thing, or you are a 'pro-crasta-decision-maker', that is when you will start to feel sick in some way, or whinge and whine, or feel frozen and unable to take a step forward. You will feel as though your foot is stuck in mid-air, ready to take a step, but, because you don't know what to do next, there is nowhere for the foot to go …

I have a couple of suggestions for that foot … but that is for a later chapter – ha ha.

GET CLEAR ON YOUR OPTIONS

Second, it would be helpful to see how many options we are looking at. Quite often there is a decision to be made but, because we feel as though we have too many options, we decide not to look at any of them … have you done this? Sometimes, even though we feel like there are "1000" options, you can really boil them down to maybe three that would make sense. So write them down. To begin with, write down all the options until you know that you have them all out of your head; then look at them and highlight the top three options.

QUESTION YOUR OPTIONS

Next, look at those three options and do a "What if I did, what if I didn't" game with them. While you are doing this, let the idea of the option sink into your body and see where you can feel it. In your gut? In your head? In your heart?

A generic option would be:

What if I stayed doing what I am doing?

What if I didn't stay doing what I am doing?

Ask these questions for each of the options and see what you are really thinking.

Then, let's say that you decide that you don't want to stay doing what you are doing, then a decision (the first decision of many) is made. Well done. Without first making that thought a reality, you can't move forward.

Take a deep breath, let it go. Onwards ...

TAKE ACTION – BOOM!

As you start to plan, prioritise, consider and implement the new direction, be mindful of your mind, your thoughts, your gut reactions; question everything as it happens.

A few helpful ways to question yourself are:

Do I want this?

What am I willing to do differently to get it?

Where am I feeling the fear and how can I shift it?

Don't get stuck at this point and question yourself into fear and failure. We have all done that. We decide what we want, and why it is important, and then we let our doubts creep in. Please refer to the title of this book at this point – say it out loud!!

Look, I am not saying that all quick decisions are good decisions, but without somewhere to go, you are stuck, and being stuck is an icky feeling that doesn't help you to see the options. I have made some brilliant quick decisions and some that have lost me the shirt off my back.

BEING DECISIVE IN THE FACE OF DANGER

When I was 26 years old, I decided to move to Australia from the UK for six months. That sounds exciting doesn't it? I had just been made redundant from a dream job, I could do ANYTHING and that level of freedom and choice was daunting to me. But my first thought was, if I can do anything, I can do that from anywhere. So I packed my bags.

I was sitting in my little lounge with my bags packed when my Mum called me and told me to turn on the television. Back then (if you can even imagine it!) we only had five channels on the television, so it wasn't hard to turn it on and be looking at the same thing that she was. I asked what I was looking at and why she wanted me to watch this film right now. She said it wasn't a film. ... I was watching where the first plane had just hit the Twin Towers in New York; and as I watched, the second plane hit. It was September 11th 2001.

I was frozen to the floor, I couldn't think, I couldn't move, I couldn't believe what I was witnessing. The horror, the fear, the ... oh my goodness wait ... I'm about to get on a plane. My Mum asked before I could think it. "Are you still going to the airport?" I didn't hesitate. "Yes."

If I had left space for too much thought, the fears would have set in, and I couldn't let that happen. I was being picked up in an hour to go to the airport. I rang the airline, I rang the airport, they said that the only flights leaving at that moment were to Australia, so yes, it is still going.

My friend arrived at my front door and looked at me – "Are you sure?"... "Yes." I had been over the "What if I did, what if I didn't" questioning in my head. I decided that if it was going to happen again, it's going to happen, I can't stop it, I don't have control over it.

I started saying to all the people that called me "If it's going to happen again, it's going to happen, I have no control over it". "I can't stop doing what I want to do because of something that MIGHT happen", and that made sense to me. Because I was set in my decision, there was no room for more negotiating in my mind. I had made the choice and I was sticking to it – not at the expense of logical thinking, but at the cost of if not now, when. Looking back, it wouldn't have been the same part of my story if I had given up at that point, let all the fears and doubts from others (and myself) creep in and not gone on that day.

I got to the airport and there were tanks at the front door, the army walking around with big guns. We don't see things like that in the UK. The airport was rife with fear, tears and trauma. Don't get me wrong, it wasn't that I didn't have fear, or shed tears, or feel what was going on around me, but DESPITE all of that, my decision was made and it was the right decision for me to change something.

My friend turned to me and said, "What if you regret going?" and I said something that will always be with me and is something that I live by … ready …

"I can't regret something I try" – mike-drop! Off I went …

I stayed in Australia for 17 years – whoopsie daisy. I never regretted the choice that I made. And, with the benefit of hindsight, it was because it was such a big obstacle that was put in my way, that it made me stamp my feet and say – YES – and I did it anyway.

FOLLOWING THROUGH ON YOUR DECISION

If I look at it, it was the "top-level" decision that I made that helped me take all the steps to get there. So, my top-level decision was "I'm getting on that plane today". But to get there, I had to answer all the questions and fears of others, I had to put one foot in front of the other myself, through the fear. I had to take each step towards getting on that plane, because the outcome was landing in Australia, and I wanted that with every fibre of my being.

YES, I could have changed the flight, cancelled going, gone later, waited to see what happened next in the world, waited to see the consequences for air travel. But it wasn't what I needed or wanted to do, my life needed to start again in Australia, at that point.

That is the importance of making the RIGHT decision for you. You feel it in your bones. You know it is right for you. You know it is the right time. Then when you are questioned about it, nothing can get in the way of that outcome.

Once a new decision is made, you need to follow through with it, you need to make the plan, you need to implement and take action. If you don't, your mind goes into a stuck pattern, like a needle stuck on a vinyl record (I hope you are over 40 and know that reference!). I have a visual in my head of that now, that whirr and click as the needle hits the same spot and then starts again – EARWORM … if you ever feel like that, change something, anything to get that needle moving again, into a different groove.

You can either be a person who makes good, quick, considered decisions, or you can be a person who is happy staying where you are. It's up to you.

MAKING A DECISION

I have wonderful friends who are terrible decision makers – terrible. What I see in them are the same conversations that pop up all the time about the same things that haven't changed. If this is you, it's ok if you recognise yourself in this, it isn't a bad thing, AS LONG AS you are happy with not changing the things that you are talking about.

Try to do something different with the little things first. For example, where do you want to go for dinner? Your normal response might be something like, "Oh, I don't know, we could go here, but we didn't like it last time, or we could go there, but I was cold in that seat, or the other place, let's look at the menu and see if we like it" etcetera etcetera. Now, because that is not how I approach things, if I need to decide where to go for dinner, I decide and then deal with the wonderful consequences (sometimes, they may not be so wonderful, but still, a quick decision stops the angst). So try with the little things to make a quicker, bolder decision and see what happens.

Making the very next decision doesn't need to be epic, but it does need to be decisive.

THINGS TO DO DIFFERENTLY:

1. Bring awareness to the fact that there is a decision to be made
2. Write down the options
3. Question the options
4. Plan and take action

4

HOW TO TAKE A COMFORTABLE RISK

S ounds like an oxymoron to take a "comfortable risk", but I realise that this is what a lot of people who I have interviewed on the "Doubt~less" podcast do. They find a way to get over, around and through the doubts that may be in the way by feeling as though they are taking a risk, but thinking that the risk will be worth it.

Here is how I look at risks in a visual way. I am at the top of a cliff and I am walking around the top of it in circles; those circles are getting nearer the edge as I start seeing the options and making the right decisions. But the right option for me is to step off the cliff and see what happens. At this point I could either step off and fall, or step off and fly. I could step off and fall a little bit to a safety net and find I'm wearing a harness, or I could fly and find that I have a hand-glider attached, so the flying isn't as hard.

I hope that that helps the visualisers amongst you and also gives you a barometer of where you might be sitting in your comfortable/uncomfortable feeling of taking the next risk.

WHY DO WE NEED TO TAKE RISKS?

The very short answer to that question is – you don't. But without taking risks you are staying in your comfort zone, you are staying where you are now, doing what you are doing now, having the life or business that you do now; and if you are happy with that, then that's no problem at all ... move on to the next chapter in the book. But what I have seen from working with hundreds of business-women over the last 14 years is that the next step is shrouded in taking that next risk and sometimes, until you take it, you can't see the potential of what you are capable of. Sometimes, unless you take that risky next step, even though it's shrouded in uncertainty, you won't be able to release your potential and discover just what you are capable of achieving.

What came first? The success or the risk? A little chicken and egg humour. Mostly (I would even go so far as to say 99.9% of the time), you can't have success until you have taken a risk, however big or small that risk is, and whatever the scale of that risk looks like to you. For instance, for some that risk is a financial investment, for some an emotional investment, for others it is a visibility risk that feels so scary, it keeps them playing small in their business.

Actually taking that risk can feel as though you have been wearing an all-in-one bodysuit (it's bright pink by the way!), and suddenly you are busting out of it and finding yourself in the process of becoming more you.

We need to take risks to find success and as you move through your life or business, you will see that each new level or incarnation comes with its own set of risks that are sent to ask us the question, "Do you feel lucky punk?" – or something like that.

HOW TO TAKE AN UNCOMFORTABLE RISK

How to take an uncomfortable risk... and make it more comfortable. If I told you that you could very easily take more risks, and that those risks would be wrapped in bouncy cotton wool and feel squishy and comfortable, safe and secure, would you take more risks?

That feeling of cotton wool cocooned risks comes from creating and sticking to your boundaries.

What are the boundaries that you have in place now for your personal and business protection outlining what you will and won't accept? For instance, if someone said to you "Give me 50% of your business and I'll make you a millionaire", would you leap at the opportunity, or would you say very quickly, "No thank you"? Neither of those answers are wrong, because at that point, you have no idea what the outcome will be or the process of what it will take to get to the outcome. This example is to see what your gut reaction would be in the first consideration.

Here's another example. I am very much an introvert; people don't believe that, but I am. I need time by myself to gain the amount of energy that I need to put out there for when I am "seen". So if it is a Saturday morning and a friend of mine says, let's go out tonight, then my instant answer is NO. For me that is a risk to my energy and, as much as that might be a really fun night, it isn't what I have planned for and so my boundaries say NO.

So, how do we take an uncomfortable risk? It is that heartbeat of time in between hearing the risk and answering the question. Even if the question is in your own head. In that heartbeat of time, there is a moment to evaluate the risk and give a considered answer; even if the answer is "Give me time to consider my answer". There is a difference between NO as a fear response and NO as a clear boundary answer. The strength of conviction comes from that Yes or No that has your boundaries to back it up. Can you hear the difference? If you say No as a fear response, then it is shaky because you can be persuaded to change it, and that won't help you when you feel like you are potentially going to take a risk. You need to build that risk on solid ground, and that solid ground is built on your vision for the future, the goals that you have in place and the boundaries that align with who you are and what you want.

Now THAT sounds like a solid place from which to take a risk .

WHAT IS YOUR LEVEL OF RISK?

Throughout my life, I have been one of those full-steam-ahead, audacious, all-out, bull-in-a-china-shop kind of people. (I've calmed down a bit now!) I have taken massive, and not-so-massive, risks and, the more comfortable it feels, I find myself shouting "Gimme MORE". So my level of risk taking (hello, jumping out of a plane at 14,000 feet for a skydive, I did a running jump out of the plane – woo hoo!) is high. How do you determine what your level of risk is?

Your level of risk may be even higher, or it may have sent you to the fainting couch just reading my level of risk! Everyone is different. And this chapter isn't to say, find your level and then change it; it is to say find your level so that you know where you are now and IF you need to or want to change it.

So let's say that you are sitting there thinking about this now, and you are thinking about the risks that you have taken in the past, the huge steps forward you have taken in your life and business. You are realising that taking risks is different for everyone and your level of risk might be considered quite low, and that is keeping you feeling safe and secure and in your comfort zone, but in your heart-of-hearts, you are wanting to create/be/do more … what do you do now?

What we don't want is to look back at our lives and think that we missed opportunities because we weren't willing to take a risk. We don't want to have regrets – remember in Chapter 3 when I said, "I can't regret something I try"? Well, what about if we look at those risky opportunities and say … I'm going to do it. SQUEAL … how does it feel … exciting, terrifying, nervous, exhilarating, all those things, but is there somewhere in you that WANTS to do it? If it is a hard no, then move on, let it go, but if there is a little spark of curiosity, then let's explore that! In JUST doing that step, you may have found a new level of risk, but let's put a little cotton wool around it. IF you were going to take that step, that risk, what boundaries, goals and expectations would you want to have in place to protect yourself?

Consider the potential outcome if you looked at the risk with a plan in place. It doesn't feel as daunting does it? Well, does it? Consider not taking that risk and missing the opportunity. How does that feel to you?

OK, it may feel daunting, but do you want it? And if you do, then how do you find the goals, boundaries and expectations that will make it feel more solid for you?

LET ME COUNT THE WAYS ...

The options are endless and far-reaching for you to build that solid ground. The trick is to look for what you need and KNOW what you need.

At every turn of my business growth, I have had a different business mentor who has pushed and supported me to make the bigger decisions and take the bigger risks.

Throughout my whole business life I have run and attended networking events; why? Because it puts me around other businesswomen who are all going through the same thoughts. We get it. Also, at those events are my ideal customers, so talking through ideas, risks and services is really helpful because you can see first hand if something is worth your time and energy.

Attending mastermind days to get hot-seating, where you have an amount of time to talk to a room of businesswomen who are on the same level as you and want more ... that wanting more is really important; investing in these days can change the course of what you thought was possible. I have run these mastermind days for years, because the impact is profound. The feeling that you can do anything is immediate. This isn't to say that it is all jumping up and down and rah-rah. You get the time to pull it apart, and put it all back together in a way that benefits what you want.

As far as conferences are concerned, imagine being in a room of speakers who have already done it, taken the risks, done the work and seen the outcomes, that can be so encouraging for you to witness the potential.

And retreats – both health retreats and business retreats. Take yourself out of your normal day-to-day routine for a few days and concentrate on YOU, without the distractions of everything and everyone else. Clear your mind and fill it up with all the good stuff that gives you the confidence to say YES to that next level.

A REVERSE RISK

I had a client recently who took a big risk in changing her business structure, but the outcome was the opposite to the growth that you might expect.

She has spent the last 18 months working on an online course. She knew that it was needed by people, and she knew that there was a gap in the market. All sounds peachy, yes? Well, no ... once she was at the stage of launching it, it just didn't feel right, it was draining her of her valuable resources, her time and energy. It was aimed at a market that she wouldn't have the capacity to support in the long run. When she started the journey of creating the course, she was so excited about it, it all came easily to her, so she took the risk and did it. It energised her to think about it, create the content, think about the customers who would benefit from it ... and then things changed.

Her life changed at home, her bread-and-butter business was suffering because her time was taken. She began to realise that the course wasn't going to happen. The thing is, that feeling of "This isn't for me" began about eight months into the 18 months she spent creating, thinking and doing. That extra 10 months was angst of "I'll just keep going because I have got this far", even though she knew in her heart that it wasn't going to launch. Then, on the 18 month mark, she decided to take the risk and STOP, stop creating, stop the energy going towards it, stop thinking about it and just let go of the whole concept of having an online course! Brave! I was so proud of her. It is always about timing and, once she made the decision to let it go, her time and energy was freed up in her mind to do bigger things with her own business.

The wonderful thing about all this is that, with hindsight, she can see she has some incredible content, all of which can be repurposed in different ways through her business. And in both taking the risk to build the course, AND in taking the risk in stopping it, she learned to trust her gut instincts and trust in herself more.

WHO DO YOU NEED TO BE?

A different way of looking at risk is asking yourself, who are you now and who do you want to be? If you are perceived as a person who doesn't take risks, then how do you change the perception, for yourself and for others, that you are open to considering new possibilities and opportunities?

It is all in the language that you use. Both in body language, "Be careful what your face says" language and verbal language. Let me explain.

If you are asked to take that step off the cliff – do you jump back from the edge and fall to the floor? Does your face contort into the face of fear and internal (or external) screaming? Do you shout obscenities and verbalise the madness of the situation? If any of those might be your reaction now, then how do you want to handle it differently in the future?

Again, we are standing and looking at taking that step off the cliff. Your body takes the step, knowing that you are safe in your boundaries and that this is not going to hurt you, so you take the step and look for the net. Your face smiles and stays in a serene state of acceptance. You say "I can, I want this, I'll do it".

Or something like that – there may be stages in between the contorted face and the serene face!

The point I'm making is, change can happen. Risks can be taken. Steps can be put in place to help you feel safe and secure. Support is out there when you are willing to look for it.

Don't stay IN your comfort zone, if you know that you are meant for MORE.

THINGS TO DO DIFFERENTLY:

1. What is the next "risk" that is on your list that you want to approach?
2. Check on your boundaries. How are they building your solid ground for risk taking?
3. Decide what your level of risk is.
4. What is the potential outcome from taking a risk?
5. What and who do you need to do/find/be to take the risk?
6. What will you learn from taking the risk?
7. Plan and take action.

FIND THE PEOPLE WHO FUEL
YOUR FIRE

DROPPING THE MASKS AND BECOMING VULNERABLE

L et me tell you a little story to begin this chapter. As I mentioned in Chapter 1, my sister Jody died when she was 33 years old. She had cerebral palsy, and she and I had a wonderful bond and relationship, it was very special. So losing her took a part of me with her, I felt a massive void, a Jody-shaped-hole in my being. I had never known grief before and I didn't know how I would ever feel like myself again. And that is the wonder of this bit of my story. I never did feel like my old self again – but, believe me, that is a good thing.

I didn't know that I needed the change, but in Jody's loss, she gave me another gift. The gift of being vulnerable. I didn't know what vulnerability was, I had had it covered up so deeply by showing up with my bravado and cocky-confidence in my corporate career. I had just started my own business, about two years before and I was still showing up as my old self, thinking that "that was how business was done". I even showed up to a branding photoshoot in a black suit ... on a beach ... with a bunch of daisies ... totally didn't know who I was in those days. For anyone who knows me, or has seen my business now, I am the hot-pink-lipstick-wearing-bright-clothes-larger-than-life-fun-loving woman, but in the days and months after Jody died, I felt dead inside.

I look back now and realise that I felt like that because I was in the soup stage of a caterpillar becoming a butterfly. I was in my cocoon turning to goo and metamorphosing.

So, I'm in the worst kind of grief and I remember being back in the UK and saying to my Mum, I have to go back to Australia, I have to get back to work. I felt like there was a little black cloud over my head, raining down sorrow, but I am a person of action and I knew that if I didn't want to stay feeling like this, I needed to get back to what I knew.

I arrived in Australia to much support from my lovely friends. I was also running networking events at the time and I decided to do a workshop and to talk about being productive through grief – my grief.

The reason that this story is relevant to finding the people that fuel your fire is that, when I stepped into that room, I realised that I was basically naked. No ... not literally (oh gawd please tell me I put my clothes on!), but emotionally. I didn't have the wherewithal to wear all the masks that I had been choosing all of my life. I didn't have the capacity to be anything other than just lil-ole-me and I felt naked and vulnerable; but the people in that room were like a comforting blanket wrapped around me. That told me that they were listening to me, seeing me as I was, and that that was enough. It was powerful and profound.

The Jody-sized hole in my fabric was beginning to heal through the process of finding myself and my people. And, not only that, but the hundreds of people that it would take to encompass part of that hole gave me the permission that I needed to decide not to put those masks back on. I could see that they liked me for me. I could hear them responding to the way that I was talking. I built a very successful business through being vulnerable and authentically me. Ta daaaaa ...

That is not to say that it was "that easy", I wouldn't suggest that anyone goes through what I went through to get there, but it is important to recognise the masks that you may be wearing and to question whether those masks might actually be hindering your ability to attract the right people to fuel the fire that is inside you.

Just in case you don't know what I mean by "dropping my masks", I used to be a very different person for each different person that I was around, it was exhausting. So I would be the good girl, obedient child for my parents, then the Rottweiler at work (I was called the Rottweiler with lipstick, because I got my teeth into something and wouldn't let go!), then the good-fun-girl with my friends, then the friendly-approachable Manager with the teams that I managed … I would sometimes forget to be the "right" person to the different people and get very strange looks. In my process of grief, I dropped all my different ways of presenting myself to the world … and just became. … ME.

BE HONEST WITH YOURSELF

Honesty feeds growth. If you are honest with yourself about who you WANT to be around and who fuels you, then it will be the fertiliser for the growth of your planted seeds … just hopefully not as smelly!

I have friends that I have had for 30 years, they are very supportive and believe in me, they are my people that I can turn to for EVERY-THING about me, but they don't have their own businesses and the world of small business is a different world to be in. So they can be supportive, but they can't understand, not because they don't want to, but because … they can't. Be honest with yourself, look at the people around you. Do you have the people that you NEED to be able to drop all the masks, be vulnerable, have the bigger conversations, be authentically you and be championed for what you want to do in the future?

There is a chasm between being honest with yourself and being honest with others. It takes a level of strength, vulnerability and courage that can only be fostered through finding your peeps. I have a small group of businesswomen who know me and my business inside and out. I have a small group of business mentors that I follow and work with because they give me the confidence and courage not to doubt myself, they are showing me the way. But having those small groups of confidantes and mentors comes from years of getting it wrong, trusting the wrong people, relying on the wrong friends and looking in all the wrong places for support.

My small group has developed because I got real and honest with myself.

NAME AND SHAME!

Terrible sub heading Trudy – ha ha! What I mean is, list them all out. Make a definitive list of all the people that are around you, that you interact with on a daily, weekly, monthly basis. Family, friends, colleagues, acquaintances, mentors, name them all.

Now that you have that list, go back over it and use a colour (I would suggest red!) to highlight the ones that take energy from you, the ones who only call you when they want something, or who call you to talk all about themselves and don't ask you about you. This is a SECRET list, so don't worry, it is just for you! Now go back over that list and highlight five people who fuel your fire, who give you energy, who don't doubt you, but might challenge you, who listen and give helpful advice.

Are the people different from who you thought they would be? There is a quote attributed to Jim Rohn which says, "You're the average of the five people you spend the most time with". Well, who are these people to you and, if you are the average of them all, is this enough for where you want to get to?

Again ... be honest ... this isn't just about dissing the energy takers, they are there for a reason (and some may be family members, so we can't do much about that!). But it is a question of coming back to those boundaries and protecting your time and energy SO THAT you can be and do MORE and be impactful in your life and in your business.

FUELLING YOUR FIRE

Picture the scene ... you sit down at a campsite, in the perfect set up, with your little pitched tent, the stars are twinkling, the moon is full, the rabbits have tottered in to see what you are doing ... wait ... this isn't Snow White ... but you get the picture. You have kindling for the fire ready and logs beside the fire ready to stoke it, you also have a bucket of water and a super-soaker just in case the fire gets out of control. Each of the people on your list comes to sit by your fireside to sing folk songs and talk to you.

When they leave, have they put a log on the fire of your dreams, successes and future visioning, or have they used the super soaker and put it out? AND, if they have used the super soaker gun, how badly is the fire out? Is there a flame, a spark, or just the remnants of smoke?

PLEASE consider that analogy ... because if there are people around you who are super soaking your ideas because they have had a chance to take a flame, then you need to be protecting your-self from sharing anything of any significance until it is DONE, and you can say, look what I did, rather than, I'm thinking of doing this.

Pick the people that layer your fire, give you the oxygen to grow the flames and the extra logs to keep you going.

ALIGNING YOUR VALUES

What I have seen time and time again with my clients is that they often have people around them who don't align with their values. This might not matter when you have a corporate job that you can turn up to, get paid and leave at the end of the day. But it matters a LOT to those of us who need to be able to sell what we do and be of service with our businesses. It is different.

So, firstly, work out what your values are – I'm not going to do a list of values here, but google "list of values" and see which ones resonate with you. I like to check on this each year and pick three that feel the strongest.

This year for me, one of my core values is being ethical. I see so much that goes on in the online world that doesn't feel ethical to me, and I am now quick to spot people with unethical traits and remove them from my news feed.

What values do you hold dear? And, in the list of five people you have highlighted, can you see the same values in them? Don't be worried if at this stage you think, hmmmm maybe my values are more aligned with a different person on the list – we are playing around with this and it is a moving feast.

What is wonderful (and I have witnessed it), is that once you are clear on your values, the right people will start popping up who align with your values. You will start attracting them and all of a sudden you will think about this chapter again and think – WHAT THE … well I never did … these were the people who I was inviting in, in getting clear on who fuels my fire and who aligns with my values … by the way … you're welcome.

WHERE CAN I FIND THESE MYTHICAL PEOPLE?

I run networking events, and I have so many people say that they would love to come along but … *insert all the excuses here*. They are not my people.

I need the action takers, the people who are committed to growth, the people who show up and say, "Today is hard, but I'll get through it, tomorrow is a new day", the people who know they are meant for bigger things and are going for it, through all the doubts, all the fears, all the ups and downs.

So I tell everyone who shows up to my networking events, that they are the bold and brave ones for showing up and telling us about their businesses. It is the only way that we can find out about them, and the quickest way to build the "know, like and trust" for a business.

Start there. Find a networking event and TURN UP. Networking works when you work it. You can't turn up once and say that it doesn't work for you. Show up consistently, let the right people fuel your fire, build you up, show you what is possible.

Outside of business events, go to things that you love to do. The activities that light you up, fill your cup, make you feel alive, where you will meet other people who feel the same. I have a client who is a highly intelligent tax accountant who loves to craft for her downtime. I have a friend who runs a charity and sews in her spare time.

I love to wander, I love city tours, or art gallery wandering; get me on an open top bus with an audio and I am as happy as the proverbial pig!

I found my people carefully, over time, through wheedling out the people that had forgotten to chuck a log on my fire, or had started to pour water on my little flame – and that reassessment might need to happen at each incarnation or level of your business.

The mythical five people who fuel your fire may well be in your current circles of family and friends. Look inwards before you start searching externally for all the support.

JUST IMAGINE...

You read this book, you start to do things a bit differently, you drop your masks and become more vulnerable in your relationships and in the way that you communicate. You communicate with the RIGHT people so that your fire is fanned and flames appear. You put caution tape around the people that take your energy and time. You look at your values and see where and how they align with the people that you WANT to have around you.

You feel more supported and secure to make the bigger decisions and take the risks that put you in the right direction for your life and business ...

BLISS!

THINGS TO DO DIFFERENTLY:

1. What masks do you need to drop/change?
2. Make a list of your network of people. Pick five that you want to spend more time around.
3. What are your values? Do they align with your five people?
4. Find the people that stoke your flames!

6

HOW TO OVERCOME THE LITTLE VOICES OF DOUBT

L et's be honest, sometimes those little voices of doubt are far more like loud shouty voices that block out all the positivity and make us feel as though nothing can be done because we have a high-pitched scream in our ears ... please tell me you have this too?

BE WILLING TO CHALLENGE YOUR THINKING

The first thing that we need to train ourselves to do is to listen to those thoughts, and be willing to challenge the thinking. Easier said than done, right? I first heard about doing this in a counselling session when I was about 32 years old. For all the years before that I had heard the voices and mostly allowed them to win. What I realised was that a lot of the time I could overcome those voices in a work situation because I was doing things for other people, but I didn't question them when it came to things for me, my health, my life. It was as though the doubt created a button of self-destruct, or self-sabotage, rather than a megaphone over the noise to say STOP, listen, act differently.

When the counsellor sat me down and showed me how I could think differently, I got very angry. She made it sound so simple and I felt as though I had brought this all on myself – can you hear the victim mentality? I left her office in a rampage of denial and "How dare they" voices in my head. I think it took me about a year of challenging the thoughts for me to realise that she was right. But boy-oh-boy did it take some work for me to change my mind. She wrote a chapter in her book about me, because the whole process for me was so visceral. I felt as though the doubts had to worm their way out of my skin; it felt painful, hard and lonely. At that time in my life I was working in a very toxic environment (emotionally speaking), I was on some pretty hefty painkillers for all the pain in my body, and I felt as though I was on self-destruct. If you can relate to that, then let me tell you what worked for me and, hopefully, it will give you a structure to try for yourself.

The first question in all this, is … are you willing to change? I remember answering this question with an air of "of course I am", but I don't think I really believed that changing my thinking would actually remove the little voices (or, at that stage, the apoplectic voices) of doubt.

If you can accept that you need to, and want to, change, then change starts to happen. That acceptance is the first step in being able to move towards, rather than away, from yourself.

What I realised was that a lot of my doubts were based on what I assumed other people were thinking. I can't find who this quote is from, but "Assumption is the lowest form of knowledge" rings so true here. We base how we feel on what we assume others are thinking, with no basis of truth or evidence to back it up. Then we take that assumption and let it hinder our progress. Ummmm … something is very off in that scenario!

So let's take back control of how we are thinking. If you are having one of those mind-bending conversations with yourself about the doubts and assumptions that you are having, then plant your feet square on the ground and question them, "Wait, is that thought true? Is it helpful? Does it benefit me?". When you have your answers, carry on with your lovely day. When I first started doing this, I would literally stop myself in my tracks and plant my feet down firmly, because I needed the physical action to be able to change the mental thought. Now, I have a learned and trained response, where I click my fingers near my ears, so that my brain snaps back and says "WHAT?" and then I can change the thoughts very quickly. PLEASE don't think that I manage to do this all the time, I still go down very dark rabbit holes of "woe is me", but I don't stay there very long, I can't, I have things to do and people to motivate!

BE KIND TO YOUR-FINE-SELF

Ordinarily, when we have those voices of doubt, we are bashing ourselves in some way, saying "Why can't I do this?", "Why do they think I can't do this?", "Why do I make everything so hard?" etcetera etcetera. Now, stay with me here, when you catch yourself having those thoughts, plant your feet down firmly and give yourself a virtual or physical hug. I remember watching a Billy Blanks exercise video when I was in my 20s (yes ... video ... actual VHS!) and at the end of the video he would say, "OK, now put your left hand on your right shoulder and your right hand on your left shoulder and squeeze, that's my hug for you, have a good day", I loved that. Give yourself a squeeze. The person that you are today has their own story to tell and you can be thankful for what got you here.

We also need to be willing to recognise that change is a good thing and that this change needs to come from you, so start with you, and start with being kinder to yourself. Does that all sound a bit froo-froo and wishy-washy? Let me tell you, my perpetual positivity started when I made the conscious decision to think better, kinder thoughts about myself. It stopped my self-destruct button, it poured cooling water on my anger and as the steam escaped through my ear-holes, I could breathe again.

I started saying out loud how good I was at something, I started saying what a good day I had had, I started saying more about the people I had helped and how that made me feel. I have these wonderful conversations with family members where they will say, "Did you have a good day?" and I will happily reply "I was brilliant today" and they will shake their heads and laugh "You can't say that" – to which I reply "If I don't tell myself that, who else is going to?". I love congratulating myself on a job well done, I feel like getting my pom-poms out (not a euphemism) and giving myself a little celebratory dance. Well done Trudy, you did good!

BECOME A STRENGTH SEEKER

When you run your own business you have to wear many hats, sometimes all in the same day. We have to be able to do marketing, accounts, content creation, social media, customer services and have the time and capacity to do the things that we love, whether that is making a product or providing a service. It all takes time, energy, love, sweat and (quite often) tears!

In the growth of any business, there comes a time when you need to make financial decisions about where and how to outsource some of those (let's be honest) tedious bits of the business which don't play to your strengths. This becomes even more important when you can bring logic to that thought process of, I don't doubt that I am good at what I love to do, but all the doubts come swimming in when I am doing the things that I don't want to do, or I don't know how to do, or I don't have confidence in doing. And this ... my Lovelies ... is where your old friend procrastination comes into play too!

You are an entrepreneur, a businesswoman, you know why you started this business and what you want it to achieve. And yet, you stay paddling around in the areas of the business that don't suit your strengths and create an algae-infested shallow bit of the pool for your doubts to thrive. I can hear you shouting at this book, saying, "But I don't have the turnover / income to be able to outsource yet". I hear you, and I didn't for years either – UNTIL – I made a plan to make it happen. I would spend absolutely no time on my accounts or the financial side of the business, because it most definitely is not my strength, it made me feel sick to think about what I wasn't doing, the knowledge I didn't have, the doubts that kept the whole business small.

So I made a plan to outsource it. The first step was to find out the cost, because just saying "I can't afford it" is not helpful when you don't have the information to make an informed decision. I found out the cost of the investment (because it is most definitely an investment; an investment in my mental health as much as anything else!), and I aimed to be able to do that in a period of time, then I took the actions to make it happen, and guess what … it happened. I have done this at each stage of my business and with each area of the business that I don't have strengths in.

This doesn't just need to be business. I have done it at home too. I love cleaning, I find it quite therapeutic (weirdo-alert!), but as the business grew, I didn't have time for it and it became something that I was dreading, so I outsourced it – and the weight that it lifted from my shoulders was immense, I wish I had done it earlier.

My wonderful friend Gillian Jones-Williams from RISE Empowered Women's Development Program, teaches that "If you only work on your development areas, the best you can be is aver-age. If you work on your strengths, you move towards exceptional". Wow, that hits me in the feels. Hearing that made me realise that, if you want to move past the little voices of doubt and grow, you need to be working with and on your strengths.

DESPITE THE DOUBT

I have an alter ego. Think Beyoncé's Sasha Fierce! I have the wind machine on, I'm probably not wearing a leotard, but I do have a cape and a friggin' tiara, my big girl pants are pulled up high and I have a tool belt with a highlighter and a notebook – ready for action. Her name is Daisy Doubt~less and I'm here to tell you, she can do anything she wants.

I obviously came up with the name recently, but she has always been with me. When I am scared, fretful, doubting myself, having the full-on arguments with myself in my head, then I allow her to step in and take over, and she says "STOP IT". I hope you have the visual of the wind machine blowing my hair, highlighter pen at the ready, tiara glistening in my halo (stop it, Trudy … too far!). Daisy Doubt~less can get anything and everything done in spite of, and despite, the doubts that I (Trudy) have. She is the part of me that has a voice like Thor and Mrs Doubtfire all rolled into one: caring, strong, powerful and unwaveringly supportive. Do you want one of these? I would love it if you create your alter ego and tag me on social media!

Sometimes, we just need that extra oomph to move us towards action and out of inaction. The best and quickest way through any of those little voices of doubt is to take action – at all times and in all ways, take action! And let the strength of your alter ego guide you, if you have too many of the little voices in your head. Their strength … and a wind machine … everyone needs a wind machine!

THINGS TO DO DIFFERENTLY:

1. Listen to your thoughts, acknowledge them and then challenge the thinking.
2. Be kind to yourself, think about changing how to talk to yourself.
3. Decide where your strengths are in your life or business and make a plan to outsource the rest!
4. Find your alter ego – what would she do?

7

LEARN HOW TO TRUST YOURSELF

F un fact: Trudy autocorrects to Trust ... take from that what
you will ...

So when I am typing my name, it comes up as Trust Simmons –
and I take that as a sign (I know you are testing it now ... then try
to lick your elbow!).

I PROMISE!

I think sometimes it is way easier to put your trust in other people
than it is to admit that you trust yourself. Just think of the long list
of things that you promise yourself on a daily basis that you don't
follow through on. Is that an unfair statement? I know that I do
that, so I'm hoping that you read it with compassion, not judgement. How can we ask other people to trust us, rely on us, depend
on us, when we can't be sure that we are that person for ourselves?

I see you "people pleasers" jumping up and down and saying, "Yes,
but I am very loyal, dependable and trustworthy for other people,
I'm just not good at it for myself"... and herein is the lesson, the life
lesson for growth. You NEED to be able to trust your own word.

Think about it (and this may just be me!), you wake up each morning and promise yourself that you aren't going to grab your phone the minute you open your eyes; I even set myself a reminder, "Don't grab your phone", which … comes up on my phone as I grab it – hilarious! Or you start the day saying that you will go to the gym, go for a walk, do some exercise, then all the things get in the way. Or you make the "Things to do" list that must be done today, or you commit to writing a book in ten days (total eye-roll!). And in making those promises to yourself, that not even you think you are going to keep, it sets you up for that dreaded feeling of failure, and it gives your doubts more power to say, "Well, you didn't do it last time, so what makes this time any different?".

If you are wanting to build trust, both in yourself and in others, then prove that trust is there for yourself. And please, not in an "I'll show you" antsy way, but in an "I get it, to trust myself is to build trust in others" way. So how do you do that?

Start small. What is a little promise that you could make to yourself, that you know you can keep, because it isn't dependent on time or energy? For instance (and I am definitely not promising this to myself!), I won't eat crisps today, that doesn't take time or energy, but it does take a commitment to your promise and willpower. Trusting yourself is a muscle that needs exercising to show that what you say, is what you will do.

Think about New Year's resolutions, all those promises that are made and broken within 12 days of the new year. That is the average time that it takes for people to give up on them.

So again, start small, decide on where and what you CAN do and commit to? What can you turn up for consistently? James Clear in his book *Atomic Habits* talks about consistency over intensity, and that makes a lot of sense to me; you want to be consistently showing up and proving that you can trust yourself, not doing it for an intense period of time and then stopping.

Repeat after me... I promise to....*insert promise to self here*...

INTEGRITY

We need to remember that trust is one of the building blocks for good, strong relationships in all areas of your life.

I have an innate, built-in part of my personality that trusts anyone and everyone until they let me down or lie to me. This trait has served me well in building a lot of business relationships, but it has got me into trouble with personal relationships. I trust blindly ... and this can be perceived as a naïve approach, and I say that because I have been told over and over what a naïve approach it is; but do you know what, I won't change it.

Integrity for me is being honest about who you are and sticking to your convictions and the things that matter the most to you. Integrity is trusting yourself. Doing what you say you will do. Following through in spite of the doubts. My level of integrity gives me a whoosh to do what needs to be done. It's not just doing what is right, but doing what is right for you. There is a strength in what you are doing and saying. When you can find that strength in your words and actions, there is a trust that is formed in your mind that says, "Daisy Doubt~less, buckle up, I've got things to do".

I was reading my friend Samantha Pearce's book *The Write Strategy* when I came up with the idea for this book. I was asked a question about book titles, and I wrote 'Doubt~less'. It was as though the floodgates of my closed mind opened and all of a sudden I had something to say. I knew that this concept was important to me, and even more importantly I trusted myself enough to be the one to stand on a soap box and talk about it. My integrity is in the pages of this book and in how I have run my business and in what I have seen my clients achieve when they feel supported, encouraged and motivated to move past the doubt, and do it anyway.

RESPECT YOURSELF

OK, I am singing three songs in my head, it is an epic mash-up (I love a mash-up!) of Aretha Franklin "R-e-s-p-e-c-t", Madonna "Express Yourself" and Erasure "A Little Respect". I hope you are YouTubing them for a playlist!

My question is, do you respect yourself enough to doubt yourself less? Respecting yourself isn't about not making mistakes, but it is about owning those mistakes and doing something differently for a different outcome.

How do you know if you respect yourself? I have had to learn this over the last few years. I don't think that I really understood this for myself before that. I had respect for other people, but I couldn't translate that to me. What I have learned is that, in my work, I have a voice and I want to use that voice to convey a message, and that message needs to be consistent, strong and clear. In communicating effectively, I have earned respect for myself by showing up at each step and each stage and not backing down when the doubt shows up.

What that has also done is make it very clear when I am not respecting myself properly because I'm not acting out my convictions. Maybe I can't get a handle on a conversation, or something is being said that I don't agree with – when that happens and I don't speak up I can feel the self-flagellation happening while I am stuck in the inaction of trying to take back my self-respect and control.

Does this make sense to you? I'm honestly asking because it feels like a very big topic and isn't talked about much. If we don't learn how to respect ourselves, and we don't know what that looks like, then how can we (and why do we) freely give respect to others? We are so good at the self-flagellation bit, but forget that it only hurts ourselves, and we know that "hurt people hurt people". We don't want to be one of those people, we want to doubt ourselves less and make a positive impact in the world ... right?

Today is a new day … if something happens to you, around you, or online that makes you feel as though your sense of respect is knocked, do one of two things. Use your voice, internally or externally, to correct the feeling, or block/delete. Don't do nothing. As Maya Angelou said, "Do the best you can until you know better, then when you know better, do better".

You could even do one of those posts on social media that says, "I was today years old when I found out how to respect myself – #Doubtless".

IT'S ALL IN THE GUT

You know when you say, "This just happened and I feel sick" or "I didn't get this piece of work done, I feel sick about it", well that icky-sick feeling is in your gut and there is a reason for that.

It is your gut reaction to what is going on around you and you need to tune into that and listen to it. Scientifically (and please check this for yourselves, I am definitely not a scientist!) we hear now that we have three brains: the head brain, a heart brain and a gut brain. It is described in some journals as the head brain being responsible for analysing and interpreting signals, the heart brain being responsible for emotional insights and the gut brain being responsible for action.

Now on that VERY interesting basis, is it any wonder that when we get a "gut reaction" it stops or drives our ability to take action? I know, right! So clever. Our bodies and our minds are here to protect us, it is just being able to listen to the right cues and hear the right responses to know what is right or wrong for us. It is also being able to distinguish between fear and excitement in our gut reaction. That can be done with a simple question session – is that feeling fear or is it excitement? – you will know when you ask it. It might also be nervous excitement, like little bubbles and popping candy – I love what my body does – ha ha!

Trusting yourself is fundamental to trusting others and in being able to take action through any doubts that you may have. When you have trust, integrity and respect for yourself, then the ability to hear your gut reaction will be true to you.

THINGS TO DO DIFFERENTLY:

1. What little promise can you make to yourself today, to prove your consistency?
2. What does your integrity mean to you? How are you showing that in your conviction?
3. Find your clear message that helps you to respect yourself on a daily basis.
4. Learn to listen to your gut reaction and take action on that.

8

HOW TO BUILD SELF-BELIEF

F irstly, my Lovely, I believe in you, not because I know you, but because I believe that everyone needs to be believed in and believe in themselves to become great; and you are well on your way to becoming great because you are reading this book and wanting to doubt yourself less and do more.

In the Collins English Dictionary, "Self-belief" is described as "confidence in your own abilities and judgement". So let's start there. Read it again ... then let's flip it to a question; do you have confidence in your own abilities and judgement?

BELIEVING IN YOUR ABILITIES AND JUDGEMENT

Easy peasy, the answer is YES ... right?

What were the thoughts that you heard when I asked the question "Do you have confidence in your own abilities?" I think I heard three answers at the same time: "Yes, I have confidence in my abilities and judgement", "Well, I have confidence in my abilities, but I'm not clear on my judgement sometimes" and "I've been let down by people, so my judgement feels impaired, but I know my abilities are strong". And this is where I have learned to go from that point and start to rebuild in that instant, rather than let those thoughts fester, take hold and take you down, rather than up.

When I am asked a question like that, and I can hear all those different responses shouting at the same time, it is always the most negative one that falls top of the pile of doo-doo that you are telling yourself, the one that shouts the loudest and that you take the most notice of. So, as your mind takes you on a wander, stop it in its tracks and question the thought, question the belief, bring awareness to how it makes you feel and for-the-love-of-all-things, question if it is TRUE!

How about writing a list of your wonderful abilities? View them as the gifts that only you have. See them as the way that you show up in the world and help people. Even in writing that list, are you questioning each one as you write them down? If that feels like a daft conversation that you are having in your head, write down the list that other people tell you are your abilities. What if you put your cape on and saw them as superpowers? Sometimes I do this as a visual, to help it embed in my heart and build the self-belief around it – it won't surprise you to know that I also sometimes do that quite literally! YES, I have a cape ... don't we all?

RESILIENCE

Having self-belief gives you the ability to be more resilient, and you know that you have been resilient before, therefore you know that you do have self-belief, but you need to find where it has tucked itself away for a rainy day. And, guess what, that day is today!

Being resilient means having the ability to bounce back, to recover. It feels and sounds exhausting and, at the time, it might feel as though you don't have the power, the control or the energy to "do it all again"; but do it all again you do. It is at times of low resilience and low self-belief that you find your grit, your character, your tenacity, your willingness to know where you are in the depths of it all and you make a conscious decision not to stay there.

Resilience is that part of you that screams, "Get me out of here, help me feel, do and be something more, something different" and your mind responds with the plan, the steps, the teeny-tiny differences that start to build towards the big changes. It all starts with the first thoughts of "I can", rather than "I'm stuck" or "I can't".

I know when you read this that you will know the feeling of being in the depths, but do you know how you got yourself out of there? Really think about it. You are where you are now because you did something different at that point, which built your self-belief, challenged your self-doubt and helped you to take the next step ... so what was that thought for you, and what was the next action that you took?

MID-CHAPTER-CHECK-IN:

(imagine a massive foghorn sound and eyes popping out of cartoon heads)

I wanted to be honest at this point; I have come back to writing this chapter so many times, and it is now the last chapter that I am writing – and why is that, I hear you cry?

Because I got stuck in my head about my own self-belief, thinking "How can I talk about this, and write about it, when my own self-belief is waning? How can I give tips and ideas about how to do things differently, when I'm not doing them myself?" I started and re-started this chapter, and then I realised what was happening.

Why was my self-belief suddenly knocked for this project? And how could I regain it, so that when I was writing it I was writing it from a place of truth? Herein lies the difference. I don't just want to "tell" people what to do and how to do it, I want to talk about it from my experiences, and writing this book has been one of the biggest lessons in self-belief that I have had to learn to date.

So here is what I did. I watched *Inside Out 2*, the Pixar film that is based all around your belief systems, where they come from and those little chips of sadness, disgust, shame and embarrassment that creep into them and transform those beliefs from good solid memories to tainted ones. If you haven't seen the film, I highly recommend it for anyone and everyone, children and adults, you will learn so much from watching it.

I moved out of home when I was 16 years old. So, really, from that young age I have had to create and cocoon my own sense of self-belief. For a number of years I didn't have much in the way of input from adults to help nurture my sense of self-belief, so I found it for myself.

Now, I am surrounded by wonderful adults (parents, siblings, husband) who nurture my sense of belief in myself, but sometimes that means that I don't actually believe in myself enough, and the bull-in-a-china-shop game of bravado starts as I try to prove my belief, rather than actually believing it.

So, I stopped writing, I got scared, I felt fretful, everything felt frustrating, I was squirmy in my own skin with the uncomfortable-ness of not doing the work. I can apply these feelings to any time that I have come to a point where "it is going to become real" (whatever "it" is), and I pull back. But I am like one of those toy cars that you pull back so that they can gain momentum. It doesn't worry me that I felt like that or that it stopped the process for an amount of time. I know myself, I ask myself the right questions, I allow the right timing and I can tell very quickly if I am stuck behind my lack of belief, or the timing needs to change, or I am procrastinating like a person that doesn't want the next "thing" to happen. When I can work that out, I then know what I need to do next.

For me, the quickest way to move forward is to talk to people. People that get it. I talked to my Business Mentor first and got clear on what was happening and what I actually wanted to happen next.

I did a brave live video into a Facebook group, because it is good to share and get encouragement. I know, especially in the group programmes and communities that I run, that feeling supported, encouraged and motivated is the quickest way to the next step.

But here's the rub; the action STILL has to be yours! So I did the baby steps, the chunking it down, the five seconds of courage and, in doing that, I started to write again. Slowly. Slower than before. But that is OK. As my step-daughter says, "Practice makes progress" – such a wonderful phrase that they are now taught at school.

PROVE IT TO YOURSELF!

Gah, you know when you have that first thought with a twist to your mouth and the narrowing of the eyes: "I'll show them"! The head thrown back in a maniacal laugh and the hands in fists. Well, that's not very helpful to you (but it feels good at the time … right?).

If you are trying to prove something to someone else, it can become a pattern of self-destruction; more of a "I'll prove them wrong" rather than "I'm going to do this for myself". The feeling behind it all is different, with a negative tinge.

The first thing to do is change the thinking and the thought process to a positive one, deciding what you want the outcome to be for you, otherwise the negative tinge gets carried through to the end product or service, and it takes way more energy to carry something with a negative tinge (this makes sense, right?).

So, what are you willing to prove to yourself and how are you going to do that?

Let's look at doubt at this point. Doubt can creep into proving something to yourself because it will mean turning up consistently and constantly for yourself and you may not have done that before, so your brain starts telling you "Breaker breaker, we don't appear to have done this before, reject, reject". You need to be willing and able to catch the thought process and put the tape back into the deck to start a new recording (ask your parents what that means if you are under 40 years old!).

You need to want to prove to yourself bit by bit, step by step, that you can do the things that you may be telling yourself that you can't, or where you haven't succeeded before. For instance, if you have always said that you will eat a healthy breakfast to start your day off in the right way, and then each day you get up and have Coco Pops, you need to prove to yourself that this can change. Try doing one day at a time, or amending the promise to three times a week, or finding a way of proving to yourself that you can and will make a change, and turn up for it consistently and constantly, so that it is embedded in your mind and becomes the new message that is playing when you next go to prove something to yourself.

In doing that, you will build your belief in yourself one step at a time and be able to slay the doubts in your mind.

Believe a little bit more in yourself, than you don't believe each day.

THINGS TO DO DIFFERENTLY:

1. Write a list of your abilities, the things that you offer and believe in.
2. Remember when you have been resilient before and what you did to build that into your sense of belief.
3. What is the very next thing that you could do that would help you believe in yourself?
4. What proof do you need that you can do this? Create the proof.

9

HOW TO BUILD YOUR CONFIDENCE

FAKE IT UNTIL YOU MAKE IT

I had a wonderful conversation on the Doubt~less podcast about "faking it until you make it". There are so many schools of thought around this. The conversations range between "It is fake, don't do it" through to "Best thing to do!". I am somewhere in the middle, with a proven track record that it works for me. Let me explain.

Picture the scene, you wake up in the morning and you have booked to attend a networking event that day. When you open your eyes, you haven't had much sleep and you feel as though all you want to do is go back to sleep for the day, but you have committed to attending and you know that it is a good idea for you to be there. Your confidence is low because you are not feeling your best self. You drag your body up to take the actions towards being available. You drag your mind to a "I'm doing this" mindset. You take each step to prove your commitment to turning up and showing up for yourself and your business. It doesn't mean that it is easy, but you do it anyway.

You get dressed in something that makes you feel good, you get in the car, you get to the venue ... you sit in the car and psych yourself up to open the car door and get out of the comfort zone, where you are literally in the driver's seat. You enter the room, you feel the rush of fear, nerves and anxiety as you quickly assess the room and discover you can't see anyone that you know. The event host greets you and puts you at ease, introduces you to other people in the room to talk to, lets you know that you are in the right place and you start to feel more you. You start talking to people and saying "Oh, I was so nervous to come here today" and others agree with you that they were nervous too, so you aren't alone.

You start to realise that you are in a room of people who "get it"... someone says something funny, you laugh, your nerves start to dissipate, someone asks you about your business, you hear the passion in talking about what you do and why you do it; someone talks about their business and you are interested in what they are saying; conversations begin ... and suddenly ... you see that your confidence is BACK. You took the action in showing up; you were able to fake being confident, until you actually did feel confident. You, in effect, were able to fake it until you made it. This is obviously a networking example; I have run in-person and online networking events for over 14 years and I see this exact scenario happen at every event. I see it happen to brand-spanking-new people and I see it happen to people who are seasoned networkers. You just never know what is going on in someone else's life on that day which is knocking their confidence.

In the last three years, I have had countless (yes, countless) days where I've not just HAD to, but DIDN'T WANT to, show up at my own events, let alone someone else's. On those days, where it feels as though you are walking through the thickest of treacle, the most helpful thing that has happened has been to get out of my own way, take the action and "do it anyway". I say the nicest things to myself to get me to change my mindset because I know that engaging and communicating with others helps me to see the future, rather than be (and feel) stuck in the past, or the present (in those moments).

And here is what I have witnessed; it is my little formula of confidence.

People show up, they engage, they talk, they laugh, they have fun, they start to feel relaxed, they laugh some more, their visibility grows and as their sense of self grows, so does their confidence. But the first step, always, is taking the action forward.

Fake it until you make it. There is nothing "fake" in this story; you are merely displaying a willingness to move past how you might be feeling, which is going to keep you playing small, keep you hidden and hide you from other people and potential customers, and is going to get you out there, feeling how you feel, but nevertheless doing it anyway ... step by step ... listening to the new internal voice which is encouraging you to "just take the next step" instead of "give up".

Remember, people are friends/customers/colleagues/referrers who you don't yet know. If you don't show up, they can't get to know you.

WHEN HAVE YOU FELT CONFIDENT?

Think about a time when you have felt confident. Close your eyes and really think about it. When we can create the feeling in our minds, it changes the brain chemistry (that's science!) and gives us the ability to feel as though we have that confidence, even if it's just for a moment, so that we know how it feels and it might help us to realise what we need to feel like that again.

For me, I feel most confident when I'm entertaining an audience. That sounds quite strange for an introvert (which I am!) but it gives me so much pleasure to facilitate other people getting to know each other, to make people laugh (usually at me ... and that's fine with me), and to help people learn something new about themselves by delivering content in a way they can engage with.

Let me talk you through how I got to this ... it ain't pretty ... I don't know if you heard, but in recent times we had a pandemic, and all in-person events were shut down for a few years, so everything was online. Me, being me, wanted to start hosting the in-person events as soon as we could, because I missed seeing people, being in a room with people, feeling that different level of connection; but I was scared to. So what was a girl to do? I went back and forth in my mind-conversations about being brave and showing up – and then whizzed back to "No-one will show up, there is too much risk, this isn't a time for laughter." I decided that the second way of thinking was all a crock-of-phooey, so I "did it anyway". I took the baby steps, I chose a date, I arranged a venue, I put it out to my audience, I had people saying, "not yet", but I had a what-I-call, beautiful bunch of businesswomen who were dying to turn up, start to get out and wanted to get back to the new-normal. So, on I went.

It got to the day and I was a wreck – what was I thinking? So, I had to change my mindset to one of feeling more confident. I started with seeing myself at past events, with people engaged and having fun, whilst meeting new people and feeling safe and secure. I pictured me being hilarious (not difficult – 😉).

I pictured the outcome for the people who would show up on that day, and why it would be worth them showing up, let alone me showing up for them. In picturing that outcome, there was no question in my mind that it was the right thing to do, my confidence returned, I felt stronger in my stance, I felt empowered to do what felt right to me. I went from feeling like a wreck (and a nervous wreck at that) to feeling confident in the space of maybe 20 minutes. For me, it requires the ability to see the fear, recognise the fear, know that it isn't how I want to feel, make a choice, take the action and change it. That sounds easy, but it isn't, it takes practice and a willingness to practise and practise so that it becomes an automatic action.

ARE YOU TELLING YOURSELF YOU ARE CONFIDENT?

It breaks my little heart when I hear grown women say, "I'm not confident", not because it may not be true in that moment, but because it is so obviously a phrase that they tell themselves a lot, or/and one that they have heard from others and they are repeating it to themselves – "Oh yes, that is why I can't do "this", it's because I'm not confident" – baloney!

If that is a part of your "script", then how on earth can you change the years of conditioning that keeps that story playing in your head?

Firstly, be kind to yourself and decide that this is the moment to change that thinking. Secondly, be willing to practise that change, be willing not to get it right all the time, but to remember that there is always next time to practise again. Thirdly, consider that words are powerful in changing your mind, and so are the actions that follow those instructions. My favourite saying is by Henry Ford: "If you think you can, or you can't, you're right." So, if you are used to saying "I'm not confident", then you need to start to practise saying "I am confident" and then take the actions to prove that to yourself (not to anyone else).

"How do you do that?" (I hear you cry in unison). It is that old adage of affirmations; say the positive things out loud, so that the negative can't be heard as loudly … have you tried it? There is a wonderful, heart-warming video on YouTube of a little girl standing on the vanity unit in her bathroom, saying her daily affirmations ("Jessica's daily self-affirmations"). If only we had all learned this as children. Even if we didn't, it doesn't mean that we can't start right now. Make a decision about what line of your story you want to change, then make a conscious decision to do something differently and then do it!

Some examples of phrases that I hear all the time are:

"I can't do this" – change it to "I can do this", or "I can do this, but I need help", or "How can I do this?"

"I'm not pretty enough" – change it to, "I am exactly who I am supposed to be."

"I don't know enough" – change it to, "I know more than the average person about this and it is my passion."

"I don't know how to do this" – change it to, "I need help and I will find a solution."

"I'm not confident enough" – change it to, "I can feel more confident and show up for myself."

You can always Google "list of affirmations" to get some more examples that will help you.

Remember – You are enough.

'Nuff said!

EXPECT THE BEST, PREPARE FOR THE WORST

I have had conversations with hundreds of women over the last few years about where their confidence (or their sense of confidence) comes from, and the answer I hear most is "From being, and feeling, prepared".

What I then hear are all the reasons why it is hard to prepare, and the reasons why preparation takes too much time – and that they then don't feel confident. Don't you just love the way our minds work!

So, what I do in all things is start with the BEST. I create an expectation in my mind of all the good things that will happen, all the ways in which the event, the meeting, the Zoom call, the first date, will go brilliantly. Not because I am being cocky or because "I expect, therefore it must", but because if I expect the worst, then believe me, the worst will happen – what we think, we create. I start with what will go right, the best outcome. If we are going to play with "what-ifs" then let's start with "What if it all goes to plan and I get the outcome that I am working towards?" – woo hoo! Now, as I start planning and organising my thoughts and my to-do list towards that, I allow the other "what-ifs" to have a moment of time.

Let's say that I am arranging a wedding (yes, let's say that!) and I know the date that we want, I know the venue that we want, I know the people that we want, then I prepare my thinking as if all of that is in place. If I then need to reassess any of those things, then that is a new question and outcome that I can deal with at the time, but my first picture in my head is that it is all going to be OK. I expect the bestest. In doing that, when all the thoughts, fears and negative expectations are verbalised around me, I have confidence in my expectation that what I want to happen will happen, OR, if it's necessary to change some aspect of it, then I can make real decisions from a different place, rather than one of fear that "none of that can happen".

By the way, for context, we got engaged on 31st December and the wedding date, the venue and the wedding guests were all arranged in seven days (by 7th January). We got married in May with everything and everyone there, and it looked and felt exactly as we wanted it to.

Expectation set, everything else moves to make it so.

I am so often told that I am "crazy" – "You can't get that done, that's crazy", "why do you put these deadlines/pressure/ideas out there, they are crazy" to which I say … watch me!

Just for completeness, I'm not a fool (mostly, you will make your own judgement by the end of this book!), but this way of thinking is how I work best, to get the best and most exciting outcomes for me and my family. I absolutely expect the best and make preparations for "other options" (I don't like to say the worst). For example, we had to change the ceremony room at the venue three days before the wedding – that was fun! But I took it all in my stride because everything else had worked out, so I knew this would too (and it did).

If ever you need a little extra pep-in-your-step, find your go-to song for feeling more confident. One of mine is "I have confidence" from *The Sound of Music* – it never ceases to make me feel as though I am swinging that carpet bag and starting something new and exciting.

My other go-to song is Katy Perry's "Daisies", for obvious reasons - but the lyrics tell me that I am one in seven billion, why not me? And honestly, I agree!

THINGS TO DO DIFFERENTLY:

1. Where do you need to show up more?
2. Practise how to find your level of confidence – when have you felt confident in the past?
3. What are you telling yourself now? What affirmations or positive ways of thinking can you change?
4. What is the very best outcome for what you want to happen?

10

HOW TO ASK FOR HELP

(AND ACCEPT IT!)

You are superwoman and need no help – Hurrah! How dare I insinuate that you can't do everything, all by yourself in your business and your life and have it all? You know I am joking ... to try to do it all is exhausting. To do it all is exhausting, but instead of asking for help, we wait to be offered and then say "I'm fine, thank you". I know you understand this. So how about we change the narrative, change the expectations we have on ourselves and bring in all the help that we can muster, so that we can feel like we have a support team and we aren't doing this alone. Ready?

LOOK AT THE PERCENTAGES!

Here is what I hear all the time in my communities of business-women. "I'm not giving my children 100%" or "I'm not giving my business 100%" or "I'm not giving myself 10%" (not a typo!).

The thing is, we are spread thin. The level of responsibility that is socially placed on our shoulders is immense. On top of that, the level of responsibility and expectation that we place on ourselves is off the charts – it is unrealistic, and yet, what we take from that is that we are failing in an area of our lives in which we (sometimes) desperately want to succeed.

There are some hard truths in all of this. I can already hear the tutting. I can hear the "It's alright for you" that we say internally without knowing what is actually going on in someone else's life. One of the hard truths is that we can change this feeling, we can change the rhetoric, but first we need to break it down to build it back up to make sense.

If you are thinking that you need to be giving 100% to everything, all the time, you are going to fail – there, I said it.

Look at any day, week, month in your life and start with what is practical, for your life, what suits you in your circumstances. I don't have children of my own and for years the expectation was that, because I didn't have children, I was always available because I "worked from home". I was run ragged – let me change that now, I ran myself ragged. I expected more of myself because part of me felt guilty for not having children and being able to work my own hours (those hours being 24 hours a day, 7 days a week!).

I am now married with a step-daughter, so my time is split between many different (and wanted) responsibilities. I have had to learn not to be as freely available as I was before, which means that I'm harder to get hold of. People have slipped away because I can't help in the same way or get in the car at the drop of a hat, and all of that is OK with me. My boundaries are clearer. I need to put more into looking after me, so that I am more capable for everything else.

I had a client who had a small business and a baby of about six months old. She honestly thought that she could give 100% to her business in the hours that the baby slept. She calculated that she had 4-6 hours a day. Now, what actually happened was that when the baby went to sleep, she slept, ate, did the washing, cleaned the house, prepared food, made the calls that needed making, caught up on social media, had a bath, organised outings – you get the picture.

When we had our first call, I clearly said, you have MAYBE one hour a day for your business at this stage of your life. The other hours, you are needed elsewhere and if you aren't needed by the human that you are keeping alive, then you need to be looking after yourself so that you are more able to cope with everything going on around you. Just with someone else pointing this out she was able to see that the expectation that she had put on herself was making her feel useless, and she wanted to be and feel useful. Where do you need to relook at the actual time that you have available?

What percentage of reasonable time do you have for the activities, responsibilities that you have? Make a list of them and work it out. It will show you where and how to recalculate where you need to.

TIME-BLOCKING

Have you heard of time-blocking? Some of my clients love it, some find it too restrictive. Let me tell you the two ways of using it to help you make the most of it.

You know what you need to get done in a week, I'm not going to start listing all of the things that you need to do on a weekly basis, everyone is different, this is about you working out what works for you.

Time-blocking can be done in one of two ways, either to create a schedule of what is to be done and when, or a routine of the areas of your life.

To create a schedule of time-blocking, you want to look at your list of to-dos and schedule the time in your diary to do each of those things. Be specific. When you do this, you are better able to see where your time is going and how long some tasks take. This may also mean that when you can see this, you can also see where you need help. On this schedule put in the things that you *want* to do and the things that you *have* to do e.g. pick children up from school, make dinner, go to the dentist, go to a networking event.

To create a routine of time-blocking, you may put amounts of time in your calendar for bigger areas of what you expect. For instance, from 9.30am-12.00pm Work. Then you can add in a weekly layer on top of this i.e. Monday marketing, Tuesday finances, Wednesday content creation, to be completed in your work time. This clearly helps you to create a routine for moving things forward. It might be that in doing this, you see which areas you always "find other things to do" – which would encourage you to think about outsourcing that area, so that it doesn't fall to a level that means it isn't getting done. Just to be clear, those areas mentioned might be once a month, rather than once a week, but it is creating a routine for your success.

I love talking to clients about the difference between schedules and routine, because it gives us another way of looking at things as an individual rather than being *told* what is right for us. A schedule is more specific; very deliberate tasks that tell us what to do and when to do it, for example, "Go to the gym at 8.00am to do legs", "Create social media posts for 1 hour at 9.00am".

A routine, on the other hand, gives us more breadth for broader subjects and says what we want or need to do in that time, for example, "8.00am Exercise", "10.00am Marketing for 2 hours". In deciding if we want to stick to a rigid schedule or a broader routine, it allows our minds to be clear on how we better react to our list of "things to do" that are ahead of us and, even better than that, it gives us the ability to get to know how we are more productive by how we tell ourselves what to get done and by when.

HELP ME PLEASE

We have been taught that asking for help means that we can't cope, or we are weak, or that it proves that we can't do it all. As I said at the beginning of this chapter, let's change that rhetoric to a more positive story. What if we show that asking for help can be the strength of our futures, maybe it will show someone else that they can ask for help too.

Those wistful days that we sit wishing, waiting and wanting for someone to whisk us up and make everything ok. That we would love for someone to say, "Can I help with that?" and then do it. That day that we just want to go back to bed and sleep, but we tell ourselves we can't because *insert the list of to-dos here*.

I hear you.

At the crux of all of this, especially when you are in the depths of feeling like this, is telling someone, speaking to someone, asking for help.

First and foremost, is the asking for help; but then, here is what happens:

You: "Hello friend, I am in total overwhelm, I feel icky, I just want to go back to bed, I'm tired but I have so much to do that I need to keep going."

Friend: "My lovely friend, you do so much, you work from home, just go back to bed for a couple of hours and then start fresh."

You: "I can't do that, I have client work that needs doing, the dishes are piled up in the kitchen from breakfast, I have to pick the kids up in three hours."

Friend: "How can I help?" or "What do you need?" – or, God forbid, the conversation that turns it to being all about how tired they are and what they need.

Be clear in these conversations if you just need to vent and be listened to, rather than fixing; but also be clear if you are looking for help with something.

We can have these conversations and leave them feeling worse if we aren't clear with what we need, and we need to be able to have these conversations with the right people, the people that know to listen and not fix, or the people that can listen and fix.

So, picture the scene. You have that lovely conversation and your friend says, "How about I pick your kids up from school and keep them for a couple of hours for dinner, so that you have more time to do what you need to today". What is your first response? "That's fine, no thank you" or "YES PLEASE, that would make the world of difference".

Imagine that lovely friend that you are talking to who says, "Don't worry about dinner, I'm making a massive lasagne, I will bring some over for you". I have had that happen. Living by myself during COVID, in a little apartment, hadn't seen anyone in months, rang a friend (who has three children and a business by herself) in a complete pit of despair and rather than just listening and doing a Sybil Fawlty-type "Ohh I knnnooowwww!", she was already making dinner for her family, so she packed up three giant pieces of home-made lasagne in separate containers and I didn't need to think about cooking for three days! I then told her to sell that lasagne, it was the best I have ever tasted! THAT is real help.

And this is the difference between asking for help, receiving help and accepting help. We might ask for it in a roundabout way, but are we really willing or wanting to accept it, if and when it is offered? And can we receive that help without feeling guilty, and thinking that we owe them something?

Gah... we are such complex little beings.

Think of this; you are sick, the kind of flu that sends a normal person to bed for four days, but you "don't have time for that", so you plough on, you push forward, you make it last for longer because you don't rest. Someone says, "You poor thing, do you need anything?" and you say no (of course), but what you actually want to say is "Yes, can you bring me a Lemsip with honey, vacuum the lounge, put a warm flannel on my head, contact a couple of clients to tell them of my malaise, make dinner so I don't have to get up, and then watch *Friends* with me so that I don't feel so alone".

Your friend might say, "I can't do all of those things, and I don't want to get sick by sitting next to you (rude!), but I can bring you dinner and Lemsip and leave them at the front door?". You (as a friend) know that you would do the same for them!

What we so often see is the "What can I do?", rather than the "This is what I am going to do". Think about when you do this too. Do you need to think about how and when you help others, so that others are more aware that actions speak louder than words in these situations.

Be willing to accept and receive the help. Don't be a martyr, which will be to your own detriment. Strong words I know, but I say it, because it is what I do. "Suffer in silence" is no longer acceptable behaviour.

If you have your own business, you don't have the time to suffer, so ask for help.

There are so many resources and communities out there so that you don't have to feel alone, so make sure that you are using them. Asking for help is not whingeing. Ask with purpose, be willing to invest, accept and get the next thing done.

Be willing to reassess. I talk about this quite a bit in this book. There is some kind of stigma that says reassessing is connected to failing, but I say, absolutely not! To reassess is to know your limitations, understand your time, create better boundaries and be willing to say, this is what will work for me.

WE ARE ALL SUPERWOMAN

I remember seeing Denise Duffield-Thomas (very well-known Australian Money Mindset Mentor) do a social media post and a blog years ago about getting a cleaner: "I'm a self-made millionaire and this is exactly how much help I have at home". I loved reading it because, at the time, I was living by myself, with a thriving coaching and mentoring business, but I was still trying to do all-the-things.

I read that blog and hired a cleaner the next day. Why? Because, not only do I value my time, I value the time of people I invest in, which helps them to grow their business in a way that suits them. If it takes me three hours to clean my house and sweat it out and feel exhausted afterwards, is it worth my time to do that, especially if it is something that I don't enjoy and don't want to do, so that I am instantly resentful. When I met my husband, he had a lovely home with his daughter, was working full-time and cleaning the house (thank goodness he likes a clean house!), so when I moved in the first thing that I changed was getting a cleaner. It was a no-brainer for us to use our time-money-energy to get the right people to do the right job.

It is the guilt that we allow ourselves to feel when we outsource. Whether it is cleaning, ironing (who on EARTH wants to stand and iron for hours? But also... each to their own!), cooking, babysitting, nannying, driving, how far do you want to outsource, because you can!

Then there is the business side. If you are spending enough time working ON your business and not just IN your business (like a job), then where and how can you outsource? So that you are having more time for you to spend how you want – yes, how *you* want!

I have always said that I will invest my last penny on outsourcing, because I know that if something is draining me, then it won't get done and then I am getting in my own way. This might look different to you. I invest heavily in my team to make sure that I have the right people for the right job. For the jobs that I know will hold me back, keep me playing small, help me to procrastinate, tee hee.

Don't try to be Superwoman all the time! Where and how do you need or want help? Don't think that you can invest now? Make a list of the services that you would like to outsource to, find out the cost (otherwise, you are saying no without knowing if you can or you can't), know who you would like to work with and then put a timeline and a plan in place to achieve that. I would never be without a cleaner and a Virtual Assistant as an absolute minimum. How about you?

OVERTHINK AND OVERWHELM

OK, I can tell you are thinking now. Your mind is going mad with the conflicting thoughts of "Yeah, I can do that, I want to do that, I want to ask for help, invest in the services that can help me, get a business mentor to guide me" etc etc … and then there is the dramatic shaking of your head, the thrashing on the floor, with "I can't, I won't be able to, it won't work, I'll do it when *insert far off date here*". Don't overthink all of this.

Plan for it, talk it through with people that get it and take action.

Let me give you a practical example. You are sat at your desk, computer on, staring at the screen and there is something that isn't working, or isn't working the way that it should, or that you can't work out how to make it work. You sit there, looking at it, googling it, wrangling with the issue. Your mind sends you into overwhelm of why isn't this working. You feel sick, you have spent two hours trying to fix it. Then a lightbulb switches on in your mind and you think to ask for help. You go into a lovely community and ask if anyone can help – tell them that you will pay them to help you with this issue that is sending you around the twist. Twenty minutes later, it is fixed.

All that angst, overwhelm and swearing at the screen and because you thought to ask for help and supported someone else in their expertise, it is done. Let's cut that lead time down. As soon as you can see there is a problem that isn't worth your time, isn't worth your angst and isn't in your expertise, ask in your community, ask for help.

Stop thinking that everything is on you and that you can do everything and learn to accept your limitations. You will get the job done faster. Whether that is domestic or business.

ATTITUDE OF GRATITUDE

You are a wonderful person. You are not wanting to take advantage of others' kind natures, because you have that innate kind nature too. In this new era of yours, of asking for help, accepting the help and receiving it, be grateful for the help that you receive. That is the most wonderful feeling for the person who is helping (again, domestic or business) to feel appreciated. You know what it feels like when you help and don't feel appreciated or seen, so make sure that you do it differently with anyone and everyone that crosses your path.

Have the attitude of gratitude. Whether it is sending a little card, picking flowers from the garden, returning the favour, sending a quick text, let them know that it was seen and acknowledge them. That can feel even more incredible to receive when, to them, it didn't feel like much. "I was already picking my kids up, it's no big deal", but to you, it took something off your juggling plates and allowed you to spin another plate more effectively.

Say thank you, mean it and move on to your next task.

THINGS TO DO DIFFERENTLY:

1. What percentages need to change in how you are approaching your week?
2. How will you incorporate time-blocking into your week?
3. Make a list of services that you want to outsource, and by when?

11

HOW TO LET GO AND MOVE ON

Why is it important to look at how to let things go, in the context of doubting yourself less? Well, in my experience, and from what I have witnessed in clients (and people generally) I find that when we hold on to something that has happened – whether that is trauma, anger, bitterness or resentment – it becomes the thing that we focus on. And when we are focusing on that, it consumes us and we aren't making the space for the good things, the positive things, the space for creativity and joy.

What I have definitely seen is that self-doubt makes us feel insecure, and when we feel insecure we aren't able to move on until we let it (or at least some of it) go.

ANGER, RESENTMENT AND BITTERNESS

I was told by a counsellor once that anger is like drinking poison and hoping that the other person suffers the effects – but in fact it only hurts you, and the other person or people may not even be aware of how much you are holding on to.

I firmly believe, in my experience, that when you can recognise that and see what it is doing to you, you can make a different choice.

Don't get me wrong, I am not talking about the bigger traumas that can happen; I have had many of these happen in my life, and some took years, counselling, angst and anger to get over, move through and let go of them. But I do know that I have found a better version of myself by realising that holding onto bitterness and resentment was only affecting me, and that letting it go benefitted me. At all times we need to be asking, "Is this benefitting me?" If it isn't, let it go.

I have taken this to extremes, but it works for me. I can have the (what feels like at the time) biggest arguments and forget what happened the next day. I can suffer extended traumas of circum-stances and then, when my mind allows clear thought, make the right decision for me, and move on. I have told people about this and been told that this is unhealthy, that it means I'm not dealing with or facing what might be happening, that the other person wins because I don't revisit it over and over. But honestly, I've got too much good that I want to do, I have too much wonderful posi-tivity that I want to get out into the world and I doubt (see what I did there!) that I would be able to do that if I'm forever holding on to the anger in my heart.

There is a video on YouTube of a polar bear shaking. What we are told is that the polar bear has just experienced some trauma, so they plant their massive paws on the glacier and shake. They shake from head to massive foot through their whole bodies. They are literally shaking the trauma off. They shake it off. Thank you, Taylor Swift, for the earworm and the dance moves. What if you tried something different? Try acting like a polar bear and, when you can tell that you are holding on to anger or resentment, shake it off. Please note, you don't have to use Taylor's song, any song will do that is going to make you dance and shake the trauma through and out of your body. It works.

I don't want this to come across as easy. I have had to unlearn a lot of awful habits that used to keep me in the anger, and the ways that it used to come out were so detrimental to me and, unfortunately, those around me. Once I was aware of this, and made a conscious decision that it didn't benefit me, I started to relearn a healthier way that worked for me. It has taken years for me to be able to say now that I let things go very quickly. In the last few years, I have had prolonged periods of trauma, and both of the periods of time lasted for about eight months each. Both were outside of my control to make a decision on when they ended, so I didn't realise that they would last that long. Both times when they ended, I allowed myself two days of utter exhaustion as my body realised that it didn't have to fight that day; then I woke up on the third day and decided I was done with feeling like that. Then the question becomes, "What do I need today to feel better, to start to heal, to clear my heavy heart?"

I made a plan, I implemented the plan and within a week (or so) I was back to my happy and healthy self.

Here is the thing - I think in a lot of ways it isn't about whether you are right or wrong (although … you are probably right – ha ha), it is about how you want to feel going forward and whether you feel it benefits you to stay in the angry space or whether you decide to create a new neural pathway to feeling better.

One of the things that I have found helpful in this process, is replacing the negative thoughts and feelings with positive ones that look to the future. So, if I am sat here stewing over an argument, or a situation, and it is taking me down a negative rabbit hole of "Woe is me" and/or "They will rue the day". I replace it with "What do I want to feel like when I wake up tomorrow, what is the next exciting thing that I can do for myself to not feel like this, what next action step can I put in place to change the state of how I feel now?"

I've said it before and I'll say it again, I am not a psychologist, counsellor or trauma specialist. I just know what has worked for me and what has helped me to take positive steps forward to a place where I am happy with my life and I no longer dwell on the past, I look forward to the future.

But please, if you are reading this and wondering where or what to do next, remember I had nearly ten years of counselling in my 20s and 30s to be the well-rounded (ahem) person that I am today. I'm just hoping that putting some of my experience in front of you will help you to try a different approach and see if it works for you.

ACCEPTANCE AND FORGIVENESS

This is what it comes down to. How willing are you to accept how you feel, and forgive yourself? Let alone how willing are you to show acceptance for the other party and forgive them?

Remember, this is about how you feel and how you are able to show up, for yourself, your family, your community, your business. There is always a more peaceful way, if we are willing and able to look for it.

I can hear people saying, "It isn't that easy" (shaking fists at me, furrowed brows, clipped voices) – so my question is ... isn't it?

What if we tried things in a different way? Something frustrating happens. Let's say that the knives are put in the dishwasher the wrong way up (yes, there is a right way and a wrong way!). So, anger and frustration starts to rise up through you. Then you realise what is happening (conscious thought), and you decide that what was going to happen (the fire bursting through the top of your head and a voice explosion, or worse, the mumbling under the breath that no-one can hear, but everyone feels) isn't going to benefit you.

You then decide (conscious thought) to do something different and you start to laugh, laugh out loud, then you start to shake it off with your laughter, to the point where anyone around you wonders if you have stuck your finger into an electrical socket, and ... suddenly ... you feel better. The angst has been taken out of the feeling. It really isn't that big a deal, is it?

Just an example. But in doing something like this it is so much easier to see and feel the acceptance and forgiveness. You realise that it was a waste of energy doing the angry bit. It was just as easy to turn the knives around (or not ... shock, horror) and walk away to your next thing.

We are funny little beings aren't we? Just because it is what we have always done, doesn't mean that it has to be the way that things are always done. We can change, because we are human. How lucky are we?!

When we make changes to our conscious thoughts in such situations it shows we are more present to what is actually happening around us, and aware of how our reaction to them affects us.

When we get better at doing this, we are more easily able to remove the doubt from various situations by forgiving ourselves for our thought patterns and doing something different. Where we used to be full of anger and frustration, we can now replace the void with hope and belief instead. How cool is that?

BE MORE "ROSS"

There is a wonderful episode of *Friends* where Ross, Rachel and Chandler are moving a sofa up some stairs, and Ross stands there shouting "Pivot", so that Rachel and Chandler know to move the sofa around the corner of the staircase. It is very funny and became even more talked about during the pandemic in 2020 when so many people were having to pivot their businesses very quickly in order to continue creating an income.

What I saw in that time was a lot of small and very small businesses either willing to let go of the past (the past being the day before!) and change their businesses for the immediate future, or feeling very stuck in the 'fight or flight' stage of human behaviour and not knowing what to do next.

Because of this, a lot of businesses didn't survive – at least at that stage. They couldn't think or see how to pivot (or pirouette as it became known because we all got so bored of hearing that we had to pivot!). I liked the visual of putting on my bright pink tutu and pirouetting my way to a new future!

In business, and in life I think, it is much simpler to be able to adapt, be flexible, let go and pivot your way through life. We hear all the time, "Go with the flow" and I agree, as long as there are actions being taken in the direction that you want to go and towards the vision that you have for the end goal. When things like the pandemic happen, that fight or flight is a real response to what is happening around us. It is at that stage that we need to be able to trust ourselves to make some new decisions, ones that we didn't know we would have to make the day before. It is time to be adaptable with the change that is happening around us, to be flexible on the outcome that that might deliver and, most importantly, to be willing to let go of the set goal that we may have had the day before and change the goal to what is going to work for us today. And, guess what, we can do that, because it is our life, our business and we can change and let go of whatever we want to.

Letting go of what doesn't serve you puts you back in control of what does serve you. Read that again … when you feel more in control of where you are going, you are able to build your belief, build your hope and let go of self-doubt.

THINGS TO DO DIFFERENTLY:

1. What song would you choose to shake off the negative thoughts in your head?

2. Are you holding on to any anger, resentment or bitterness about a situation or person that you could let go of now?
3. Where do you need or want to be more flexible in your approach to letting go of your negative thoughts?

12

WHY TAKING PERSONAL RESPONSIBILITY HELPS OUR MINDSET

O K, let's be clear on what personal responsibility is. Personal responsibility is what you take to get the action done; it tells you what needs to be done and where it is on you to create it. It can be the little uncomfortable feeling of, "This is all on me" but it also creates the feeling of "WOW, look what I've achieved, it was all on me".

The intricacies of where and how taking (or not taking) personal responsibility can affect how we think, and what we then go and do, are far reaching. They range from being comfortable blaming others for things that could be ours to own, or sometimes giving us that tricky victim mentality, through to knowing and harnessing our growth mindset and our ability to take responsibility and own the outcome with gratitude.

ACCOUNTABILITY

When you sit up and take responsibility, you are more likely to feel as though you are accountable for the outcome of what you are creating, whether that is in life or business.

It gives you the opportunity to accept a problem and create a solution. If we can admit to mistakes and use them to learn, this can build better relationships and more trust, and that is what we all want, isn't it? To feel as though we are showing up and being authentic in a way that builds the know, like and trust in us and our products or services.

Being able to be accountable with where and how you take responsibility puts you more in control, and (I know I have said this before), control is not a bad word. When you feel more in control, you are more able to feel that you are taking action on the things that you said that you would do, you are following through and getting it done. Staying true to your word, and that is a massive part of responsibility.

BUILDING CONFIDENCE DESPITE STRESS

Remember the Henry Ford quote, "If you think you can, or you can't, you are right"? This is where we start in building your confidence, despite any stress or anxiety you may feel.

Picture the scene. You start a new business and you need a website. The thought of it puts the fear in you of what you can't do, that you haven't done it before, that you don't know how to do it. So then you start to feel the stress bubbling in your tum-tum, and the fog building in your brain, all the tell-tell signs that say, stop, you don't know how, you can't etc. What this also does is to take your feeling of responsibility away from you, it knocks your confidence from "I want to do this business" to "I don't have a website, it won't work". And in the midst of all of that internal turmoil is the pit-of-the-stomach anxiety that stops you in your tracks.

Now, consider that you are a steam train, with momentum on the tracks going up a little hill, so you need that momentum (confidence) to get up the hill and over it. As you start the ascent, the "I can't" feeling creeps in, and so you stop putting coal in the furnace, then the "I don't know how" starts talking and you shut the furnace door, then this massive train (of thought) comes to a stop on the tracks, or even worse, it starts to slip backwards because it was going uphill ...

What it will then take to get it fired up and moving again is twice what it would have taken to put the little bits of coal on and keep the engine going. I'm really hoping you are getting the point of this rather wonderful visual story. Even if and when (and believe me, it *is* if and when) you start to have a thought process of "I don't know how to do this", just work out what you CAN do. The teeny tiny steps that keep you on track, keep your confidence bubbling along, maintain your momentum for what you want to happen next. All of those moments that happen are a part of your story of what you achieved despite the stress and anxiety, and everyone loves a story of triumph.

Confidence comes from taking actions, proving where and how you are responsible for the outcome and seeing the outcome for yourself – feel your pride grow when you see that wonderful pattern for yourself.

TAKING ACTION AND FEEDING A GROWTH MINDSET

When I look back to all the circumstances where I have blamed everyone and anyone else for the situation in which I found myself, or how I felt, or what was happening TO me, I am fascinated (with the gift of hindsight) to see where all of this knowledge which I now have would have helped and benefitted me. However, I believe everything happens at the right time.

I think I blamed most of my 20s on the fact that my parents had divorced when I was 15 years old. Or that I had "left" home when I was 16 years old. Or that I got a job that was far away from friends, and I didn't learn to drive until I was 21 years old, so I was stuck.

I don't remember exactly how it happened, or when, but I will tell this story as though it was fact. "I woke up one day and decided that I needed to take action, and taking action meant taking responsibility for who I was, and what I wanted. From that day forth I did." And I don't think that happened until I was in my mid 30s.

A growth mindset requires you to build your belief by taking action. It is proving to yourself that you can trust yourself because you find a way. It is knowing that you have had to learn how to persevere and be resilient, and you have done that. You are still here and still learning. I think that a growth mindset relies on your willingness to learn and keep learning; never thinking that you know it all. If I had shut down my growth mindset in my 20s, my story would be very different, because I was a highly stressed, angry "Why is this happening to me?" person. Learning from then on the steps to take, the actions to take to make me responsible for myself and not trying to take responsibility for those around me has been a long and hard process. But, in the midst of that, it has grown my confidence, resilience and belief.

CHANGING "YOU" TO "I"

One of the weird and wonderful things I learned in taking responsibility for myself and my life was to look at why some things made me angry and frustrated and see if that was caused by something I need to look at in myself.

In my younger days, it would really irk me if someone wasn't taking responsibility for how they were making me feel – pfft … read that again – they don't need to take responsibility for how they are making ME feel – I need to take responsibility for how I feel around that person and whether it is worth my time and energy to keep doing it. AND, on top of that, it is a choice that we can see and make at any time to change the way that we view any situation. If we are saying "I can't believe how they are making me feel", how about changing that to "I can't believe how I am allowing that to make me feel".

If you are stuck blaming others, it is much harder for you to hear the victim mentality that may be driving your thoughts and therefore be able to change them.

Try starting with changing "Why is this happening to me?" to "I take responsibility for what is happening to me; where does it need to change?" A difference of only a few words, but a big difference in the approach to the situation.

It is like when you are in an argument and the other person says something like, "You did this to me". Changing that to "I did this to me" makes us take responsibility for how we feel. I am not saying that in the heat of battle – ahem – arguing, that you are going to remember all of this, but it can be a way to learn more for the future, learn more about yourself and what you can do to change, if you want to.

I don't know that taking personal responsibility is talked about often enough; maybe I don't go looking for these conversations. I do know that when you have this conversation with yourself, there is a pit of the tum-tum feeling of what needs to change, at least that is what happened to me. Once I started implementing the changes and practising (the years of practising!) the change of mindset, I felt more empowered and I could see my resilience in adversity, through the things that had affected my life to this point.

It all started with a little conversation around "Stop blaming others, where and when are you going to take responsibility?" – it is interesting to ask yourself this and listen for the answers.

THINGS TO DO DIFFERENTLY:

1. How will you remember to "stoke the furnace" rather than slipping back on the tracks?
2. Start to think about where you say "You", that you could change to "I".
3. Where and when are you going to take responsibility?

13

CREATING CLARITY

E veryone says that they want to have clarity; and everyone knows that when you have it things feel easier, but many people don't want to put the time in to gain it, realise it or find it. And so, we blindly go forward talking of the "illusive" clarity as though it is a distant thing that can't be grasped.

Let me tell you: this is my thing! I LOVE helping clients to gain a sense of clarity, because that is when you start feeling as though life and business are aligning. It gives you the motivation to move forward, having a clear picture, not only of where you are going, but why you are going that way – and of how to get there!

CHOICE VS. CLARITY

Since I left my corporate career I have had at least four different businesses that I have started, run and then changed. The last business name that I settled on was The Daisy Chain Group International Ltd, and I have run that business for 14 years, starting in Australia and then bringing it over to the UK.

Within The Daisy Chain Group, I have started, run and changed at LEAST 30 different service offerings. Why am I telling you this? Because sometimes we feel that, once we have the illusive clarity, we can't change it. That, however, is not the point of having a clear vision of the future.

You may remember during COVID, the word of the moment was "pivot". I have used this word in business for years, because we have a choice to change our businesses whenever, and however, we like – that is the beauty of running it ourselves! The choice is yours. So changing, pivoting, reviewing and refining is necessary; it becomes a part of our quarterly/yearly reviews.

What I often hear from my business mentoring clients is that, once they have made a choice, they feel as though they can't change it, because that will feel "flighty". On the contrary, I think that you can make as many choices and changes as you like AS LONG AS there is action stemming from the change. Once action is taken, the choice is clear; it is in the inaction that the clarity becomes muddied. You know that feeling of "Oh crikey, I can't see clearly, which direction do I go?" (That's in the next chapter!). Or, "I feel as though I'm walking through treacle!" Well, if you are feeling like that, then clarity and action can't happen. You need to make a choice, be clear on it and then take action.

BUSY VS. PRODUCTIVE

One of the major differences between having clarity and flying by the seat of your (big girl) pants is shown by whether you feel you have been productive, or just busy.

Picture the scene... at the end of your day, you are talking to someone and they say, "What have you done today?" – and you say, "I haven't stopped, but I have no idea what I have been doing" and then you dramatically hurl yourself on the sofa because you are so tired from all your busyness ... THAT is when you have been busy, rather than productive.

When you have had a productive day, you can't wait to list all the ways you have been productive and what you have got done, ticked off your list, completed. It feels really good. It gives you energy, rather than taking it away from you.

It is a really good practice to see and know the difference between these two things because it avails you of the opportunity to know when you have had a really good day that was just about you and your business growth.

What I have witnessed is that, when we have a busy day, it more often than not means that we have done things for other people; the little grabs of our time and energy that we were going to use for tasks for our business or ourselves, but instead we were asked to do something for someone else and we did it.

Yes, it is a choice, but also, as businesswomen (even in this day and age) there are so many extra pressures and expectations put upon us. As much as I could sit here and pontificate, saying "Don't do those things!", it would be a fib. I do it too, it is a part of life – we women are the nurturers and the do-ers, and sometimes that means that we have to sacrifice the feeling of having been productive in our business if that happens. This is not to put the blame on anyone else, or our choice, our lives, it is just fact.

And so, you make that to-do list of things that you want to do for the business the next day. You wake up in the morning to have a cracking day at the desk ... and then something changes ... a child is sick, a phone call from a friend, parents calling for a chit-chat "because you work from home, so you are always available", the neighbour needs something, the dog gets out of the gate, the holiday needs to get booked that day, the shopping needs to be done, the dinner needs to be planned. You get the drift. The list of 'other things' is endless – and so is your to-do list for your business! So what gives? Usually, be honest, it's the business stuff. Now, I am not saying STOP IT, I am just saying, be aware of it. Because, if this happens regularly, then you start to get frustrated and resentful, and you start wondering why you feel like that, and then you look at both lists and wonder why you don't feel as though you are achieving the things that you want to achieve ... and then you start thinking, "If only I had clarity"! My Lovely – I see you.

This is that mythical 'balance' that gurus talk about. We are all standing in the middle of a very steep seesaw, stepping one way or the other, with the weight of business on one side, and everything else on the other side, and being asked to make it balance. In the middle of all that is you – which can be exhausting.

But here is what I know works. When you feel like that, do something (anything!) on either side of that seesaw that is going to make you feel productive. Because when we feel as though we have done and achieved something, it feels as though the day was worth it, rather than just 'getting through it'. Clarity comes from having more of those productive days. To make those easier to achieve, try to have a list of three things that you are going to get done in a day, either for yourself personally or for your business, and get them metaphorically, or physically, ticked off!

THE BIG PICTURE

One of the questions that we find the hardest to answer is "What do you want?". It feels as though this is an endless question of possibilities and options, when actually, if we can get clear on this, then everything else falls into line.

For instance, I had a client who is a single mother of two children, who wanted her business to pay to take her children to Disneyland. Seems reasonable. Then she put all the blockers and doubts in the way as to why it wasn't going to be possible. "It's too expensive, I can't afford it, I'll never be able to afford it, I don't know when I want to go, it might be years away" etc etc. So here is what we did: we broke it down.

How much is it going to be for the trip? "I don't know, but I can't afford it" – find out the cost. For this example, we will make up some numbers; let's say that it would cost around £10,000 all in for everything to take two children to Disneyland. Is that Disneyland California, Florida or Paris? "I don't know" – find out.

When would you like to go? "I don't know, I want to take them when they are this age, but probably can't" – so we are aiming for taking them within the next 12-18 months. When we start to say things like this: "Right, so you are going in the next 12-18 months and it is going to cost £10k, and you could put a deposit down and pay off over that time" there is a frisson of excitement about the possibility becoming a reality... there is a plan in place for the big picture, there is clarity forming, so then actions can be taken.

And the actions that then need to be taken are, how can your business create and bring in that money? I am definitely not going into the tax, the expenses, the outgoings of your business in this example, but to keep things really simple, keep this in mind...

To make 10,000 in any currency, you need a product or a service that is:

1 x £10,000 = 10,000

2 x £5,000 = 10,000

5 x £2,000 = 10,000

10 x £1,000 = 10,000

50 x £200 = 10,000

100 x £100 = 10,000

1,000 x £10 = 10,000

Getting clearer now? Create the product or service that will be aimed at your audience, your ideal client, that they are going to invest in you and your business and you can create that £10,000 income for the purpose of taking your children on that holiday.

All of a sudden, anything is possible… right?

Every "I don't know" needs to have an action to find out more information to give you the knowledge that you need to make an informed decision.

Do you see what happens in that scenario? The dream, the vision, the big picture is achievable, the ideas-machine starts whirring, the cogs start turning, there is momentum for you to aim for something that is bigger than "I want to help people and be successful". A wide and general statement like that isn't a motivator for YOUR clarity.

Remember too, the example above is a short-term goal. Just imagine if you were clear on the Big Picture for your 10-year goal, and then think about what you would put in place right now to get that moving. Believe me, ten years goes past in a heartbeat, so planning for it now is a really good thing, considering, of course, that you can change, pivot and refine that big picture of how the next ten years will look along the way. You may put a plan in place for ten years, achieve it all in two years and BOOM, need to reassess what you are aiming for again!

BE CLEAR

We need to have purpose in our businesses to be able to remove the doubts (and the doubters) from our thoughts. It is so much easier to "be the snowplough", pushing your way through the doubting thoughts of yourself and others, when you are clear on the outcome, your purpose in working so hard and putting yourself on that seesaw of trying to balance "all the things".

The steps to take are simple, but take those few moments of calm and quiet that you can find to hear what you are saying.

These are the steps; ask yourself:

1. What do I WANT? Be clear on the answer and write down the things that you think of, and don't let all the "yeah, buts" and "I can'ts" come in just yet.
2. Why do I want that? Don't stop at your first response. For all our businesses the easiest cop-out response is "I want to help people". That isn't a motivator; be honest with yourself.
3. How does this align with my core values? We talked a bit about core values in Chapter 5. Go back to your values and see how they can motivate you with what you want to achieve.
4. Does this feel clear to me? If not, what is missing?
5. When this feels clear, ask yourself, "What are the very next steps I need to take?" Break it down, don't leave it as a big hairy goal that feels unachievable; break it down to the next step to take so that you are on your way to achieving it.

I would not call myself a strategist. I know how important strategy is, but I think that it is different to different people. I have some clients who love the big picture and the complete big picture strategy of how to get there, but for others this feels too daunting. They have the big picture, but need to concentrate on the next steps each month to take them to that end goal.

I am productive, an action taker and I get clear on goals, but even for myself, if a full strategy is put in front of me, I can't follow it. So 'know thyself' and know what suits you!

THINGS TO DO DIFFERENTLY:

1. What choices do you want to make?
2. Are you being too busy to be productive? Change the thinking and create what is achievable.
3. What is your Big Picture?
4. Build the plan/strategy that is going to encourage and motivate you to move towards the Big Picture.

14

DECIDING ON DIRECTION

This is a chapter that is important to me. It is what I am good at for myself, it is what my business mentoring clients come to me for, it is the bit of the business equation that makes the most sense to me, and which is often less clear for others. It gives me the capacity and the capability to say yes or no to things that are offered, and it dictates the time and energy I have for the list of "everything else".

Are you sitting comfortably? ... then I'll begin ...

Here is why one of my growth formulas (talked about in Chapter 18) consists of clarity, direction and focus. Without those things in place, it is hard to be able to bring in any strategy, marketing or progress.

THE INTERSECTION OF INEVITABILITY

Let me create a visual for you. You are out hiking, and at the start of the hike, you know where you are going to end up (if it is me, probably at a pub for a lovely lunch!). You get to an intersection of paths that can lead you up and over a mountain to get to the destination, but which one would be the best one to take? At this point in the hike, you need to make a choice about which direction to head in. There is only one direction that will get you to where you want to go with ease; the others are harder, have different obstacles and may create different outcomes/destinations.

When you make that choice, it is an inevitable outcome that is decided, so it is important to be sure about the direction you are taking. You make the choice and take the first step towards where you are going. At this point of taking the action to move, your fate is set and you need to be sure that you can handle anything that is thrown at you along the way so that it doesn't change where you end up. It sounds pretty clear, doesn't it? But this is the point where we start throwing all the doubts into our heads, comparing ourselves to other people, being distracted by "all the other things" and allowing procrastination to be our new friend, so that our foot doesn't touch the ground and it is stuck in that mid-air-action of inactivity. "What if I've made the wrong choice? What if it rains? What if I see someone else on a different path, do I change tack?? What if I can't do it? What if I don't make it? What if the lunch at the pub doesn't have chips (oh the horror!)?"

THE WAY

A little story for you. In 2016 I decided to walk the El Camino, which is a 1000km track across the top of Spain that ends in Santiago de Compostela. I was going to walk 500km of it on this trip. I had two friends who would join me for about 400km and I walked 100km by myself at the beginning of the trip. I got on the flight from the UK and arrived at Santiago to collect my 'Camino Passport' and stay the night before I got on a train and travelled 500km to start my trek. I arrived at the hotel and then completely froze.

I got so stuck in my own head because of the fears and doubts of starting the walk, let alone finishing it, that I couldn't take another step. I was pacing my hotel room, wondering what on earth was going on and why I was struggling so much. It was physically and mentally painful. I wanted to leave my own skin, curl up in a ball in bed and not leave there. And so dear readers ... I did. I talked to the hotel on the phone (I didn't leave the room) and booked for the next night … and the next night. I stayed in there for three days. By the end of Day 1, I came to the conclusion in my isolation that I was scared because I didn't know where I was going. I had, literally, no sense of direction, I was winging it and, because of this, I had no idea how many kilometres to walk each day. I also had no idea about where I was going to stay, what that would look like and whether I had the right equipment to make sure that I could get to the next town. (By the way, the right equipment was my own feet and my walking poles, so I definitely had them, it was just another excuse!) And here is what happened next.

After all the googling, panic and torture, I had a rough plan in place, but I didn't feel sure or reassured. I decided that the best thing to do was to go to the 'Camino Passport' office to find out more information and claim my Passport (you have to have the Passport and get it stamped along The Way (as it is called) so that you can prove that you have done it). So I made myself get up, get dressed and get out the door. My heart was racing, I was in a hyper-sensitive-sense-of-panic and I found my way to the Passport office. At the door was a burly security guard, who told me to stop and wait outside. I stopped dead and didn't move. As I turned to wait at the wall opposite, I saw someone that I knew coming out of the office … I was dumb-struck; how on EARTH can that happen?

Now, wait for this … it gets crazier … it was an Australian woman (Monique), whom I had met in Italy on holiday, through an Irish businesswoman, over a coffee, two months before; and she had just finished walking the El Camino over the two months between when I had met her and now. I nearly fell at her feet. She was in shock too, and as I grasped at her (I felt desperate) talking ten-to-the-dozen in fear, she looked me straight in the eyes, took my shoulders and said, "Breathe, let's get a coffee". I sat with her and she told me exactly what I needed to look out for, that it was all achievable, that it was life-changing for her and it was all worth it. I left her with what felt like renewed oxygen in my lungs … I felt ready; and so I left the Passport office, checked out of the hotel, got on the train and at 6 o'clock the next morning, as the sun was rising, I started my walk, my adventure. I took a photo of myself taking that first step because I knew what it had taken to get me there.

In taking that first step, I had chosen my direction and taken the action to start. Sometimes, starting is the hardest part, but once I was off, I was happy. I walked 500km on that trip, 100km alone and 400km with two friends from Australia. It was one of the most incredible adventures: the people that you meet, the stories that you hear, the pain it takes, the endurance, the resilience and the mindset to complete it. It was all worth it, I learned so much and appreciated every step that I was able to take. Yes my feet exploded with blisters (I will leave you with that visual!), but that story is for another time. It was 2.5 weeks of my life that I will cherish. Well worth the effort for anyone wanting to do something like this. I went back the following year and did the first 500km, I got lost, but again… a story for another time!

TIMING, RESOURCES AND TEAM

What a lovely story, Trudy, but back to deciding on your direction please!

One of the biggest lessons that I learned from what happened then was the sense of timing. If I had left to start the walk when I first arrived, I wouldn't have found Monique for the reassurance that I so desperately needed. If I had waited even ten minutes longer, I wouldn't have seen her and, without seeing her, I would have left for the walk feeling directionless, flying by the seat of my pants and scared of where I was going to end up.

Timing is everything; so if you are at a crossroads, or there are a number of options that are presenting themselves to you, give it a heartbeat to think. Is it the right time for taking action, or is it a time to see what pans out? Maybe leave a bit of room for whatever comes next – not every time, but sometimes. Think about all those times that you may have thought, "That wouldn't have happened if I had taken a different path at that time" – met your partner, got that job, started the business, bought the house ... everything is timing.

I know that every client of mine has told me they wanted to work with me because they needed someone who has also been in their position. Someone who has done what they want to do and who hasn't let the doubts and fears get in the way, but has found a way through. To me, this is direction with purpose, conviction and motivation to succeed. It is finding the right people to lean on, encourage you and say "YOU CAN", even when you might be saying, "I can't".

If you find yourself at that crossroads, thinking "But how can I get this done, how can I reach that destination?", then quite often the answer can be found in the people around you that can be a part of your team – your virtual Board members, who become your go-to resources for support.

It may very well be at that stage that you can see who you need to add to your team to get the job done; it may be specific tasks that you can't do, or don't want to do, but you know that the direction you are taking is the right one, so you find the right people to help you get there.

DELETE THE DISTRACTIONS

Picture that path about which you now have clarity. You know why you want to get to the destination, you have an idea of the team and the resources that you may need to complete the project but, as you look at the path, you can see all the distractions that 'may' become a problem and take your time and energy. Gah ... get rid of, delete, block, be the snowplough ... but with kindness and consideration – tee hee!

You need to be looking at that path and imagining yourself holding a tennis racquet and batting away the distractions so that you can feel you are being productive (and not just busy!) ... begone hour-long phone calls from family members who want a chat, sayonara to the shopping that needs doing (unless it is milk … you need milk for your coffee and tea to keep you fuelled!), ciao bella to the tasks that appear on your daily to-do list for your business – unless of course they are moving you forward to your goal.

Let me be clear, I'm not saying don't do these things EVER. I'm saying be clear on the time that you are giving to your Big Picture, be clear on the time that you are giving to your business, be clear on the time that you are giving to "all the other things" and make sure that never the twain shall meet – as in, do the things that you say you are going to do and don't get distracted. If you are spending time with your children, partner, family, then be with them. If you are spending time on your business, then do that.

It is up to you to regain control over your time and use that racquet to bat away anything that is thrown at you, with a "Thanks so much, I'm not available at the moment, but I will become available at 5.00pm" or whatever timing suits you.

By doing this, you clear your path to your destination.

Personally, I make a list of the potential distractions that might come my way so that, if and when they occur, I can be clear on my boundaries and make an informed decision on whether I have time for that distraction when it comes. Just try it, you might be surprised to find that, just by acknowledging that something is a distraction, you find it easier to say "Not now" rather than "Yes, I'll stop what I'm doing". That will stop you substituting being truly productive for just being 'busy'.

STAY IN YOUR LANE

It breaks my heart when I hear stories from businesswomen who feel stuck, or stay doing something that they aren't sure about any more, just because they are comparing themselves to someone else. The conversations of "Well, she is better at it than me, so I won't even start" or "There isn't room in the market for another *insert job title here*", makes me want to shake people and scream – YOU DO YOU BOO.

Comparisonitis is an awful affliction which stops you from going in the direction that you know is right for you. It causes you to be so busy comparing yourself to other people's so-called 'perfect' lives and businesses on social media that you forget to STAY IN YOUR OWN LANE!

To be blunt, this is of your own creation, but that also means that you have control over stopping it happening in the future. IF you choose to stop it in the future! And I really hope that you DO choose to stop it in the future because the world (your world!) needs you to be who you are meant to be. Looking around you rather than at what you yourself are doing is stopping you from being fully yourself.

I hope that by reading this book and being in my world a bit you can see that I am me, and I don't care about what others are doing. I celebrate those further ahead of me, I look up to the people who are better at things than I am, and I don't take any notice of the things that may be said about me because it isn't up to me to control what others say. Ohhhh, that was a ranty-pants, wasn't it?! But it is true.

If I hear one more person say, "There is no room for another business coach, another meditation teacher, another yoga instructor" you may well see the screamy-shouty side of me; that Daisy Doubt~less character who will stand on the nearest table and say loudly, "Hark ... I have something to say! Just concentrate on what you are doing, how you are doing it and be authentically you – people buy from people, so stay in your lane and stop looking around at ways to get in your own way, Grrrrrr." Then I will probably climb down off the table with great finesse (I don't have any!) and give you a hug.

There is a massive difference between doing market research, knowing who is in your market and what they are doing, and comparing yourself into business-oblivion and not stepping up and out to say "This is me".

That is who we want to see – YOU! Your lane is clear, you have the clarity on what is at the end of it; the distractions are now off the path and you have a clear direction of the path you want to take, so take it!

THINGS TO DO DIFFERENTLY:

1. In what direction am I heading? Is it the right time to take the steps towards the big picture?
2. What resources do I have, or do I need, to complete the project?
3. Who do I need around me in order to feel more able to move forward?
4. What distractions do I need to be aware of, so that I can bat them away?
5. Am I being the whole of myself in my business? How can I protect myself from comparisonitis and stay in my clear lane?

15

FINDING FOCUS

WISHING, WAITING AND WANTING

Years ago, I came up with the phrase, "The wishing, waiting and wanting effect". It happens when you say "I wish this would happen", or "I'm just going to wait until my 2-year old is at university before I ...", or "I want this holiday" ... but then don't do anything about it. These conversations, to me, are the most frustrating.

I have never had the option to wish, wait and want, without saying "How, when, why, what?". Because of this, I don't just "wish" for something, I either make it happen by focusing on it, or I let it go because I don't value it enough to put time and effort into it. Simples!

A long time ago I said to myself, "I wish I could move to Australia for six months" and then I made a quick, decisive decision; either I wanted this to happen, or nahhh it wasn't really for me. Because I had learned that if I do want something to happen, then you had better get out of my way, for it is going to happen and happen fast! This was able to happen quickly because I can determine the value that I put on that thought, that idea, that "wish" and then follow through with it.

Asking "How, when, why and what?" also gives you clear focus about what you want and need to do next. It creates the plan and the action steps that are needed, and can clearly be executed because you have the focus to do it.

For instance, a few years ago I was sitting on a friend's balcony. We were having a glass of something and talking about our businesses and she said, in almost a throw-away comment, "I wish I could go to Italy for three months and immerse myself in Italian culture, whilst working". Without a pause, I said, "Why can't you?". And down all the excuses came raining, all the fears, the doubts, the "I can't because ..." when actually she really, really did want to, but she didn't want to do it by herself.

Those weren't the actual words she used, but I know her very well. Both of our businesses were online, so we could run our businesses from anywhere. We both had apartments that could be rented out whilst we were away, but the list of things that needed to get done for the "wish" to happen got longer, and the feeling of "Is it worth it?" started to creep in. And, at that point, her decision was made. Yes, it was worth it.

So I put her in the car and we went to the nearest travel agent to book our flights, and then it was much easier to focus on the things that we were determined to get done for the end goal to happen. And we did. We went to Lucca in Italy, a beautiful walled city about an hour from Rome, and lived in an Airbnb whilst we worked from 5.00am -10.00am for Australian clients and then wandered the city, immersed in the culture, spending our evenings in the Amphitheatre (the square), listening to music and gesticulating a lot with our hands. It was bliss. It was an adventure. And it was worth it!

What is on your list that you are wishing, waiting and wanting to do? If you want it enough, then how can you focus some attention on it now to make something happen for yourself?

IRRATIONAL IRRITATIONS

When we can question these thoughts enough, it gives us the ability to be clear on where our focus needs to be. And when we are able to commit the time to be focused, nothing gets in our way – and if something does try to get in our way (those pesky distractions), then we may get quite irritated. (I am saying that very calmly … you may use stronger language!). It is really up to you at that point, to decide whether you are going to blow a gasket or respond reasonably with an "I am in the middle of something that is important to me, please bear with and give me another hour to complete said task, before asking me the 100 questions that you have for me" – or words to that effect and emphasis.

I have called this subheading 'Irrational irritations', which in itself is irritating … I know. They definitely don't feel irrational when you are having them, so let me explain. In all things at all times, we have the power to choose how we respond to something. How we respond affects how we feel. How we feel affects how we show up. And how we show up is important to the energy that is put behind something that we put out, be it a service or a social media post – it all matters. So in that (and back to the beginning), we don't want our irritations to be irrational, we want them to be *intentional* – ha ha. When something winds you up, it creates stress, and stress is not something that you want to associate with the joy of finally realising that you have been wishing and wanting for something and now you are taking action towards it.

So, bear with me, let's bring *intentional* irritations to our focused time. Have three phrases ready to go for the situations that are going to come and try to take your time – I swear to you, this works. For example, "Thank you for bringing that to my attention, I won't be able to look at it/deal with it/fulfil that request until after I have finished my focused task. I will be sure to let you know when I'm free". Can I hear you scream BOUNDARIES? With a choo-choo hand movement and a 'Rocky' fist-pump of "I did it". See how different that feels to being irrationally irritated, because we know it is going to happen, so be ready for it, plan for it and protect your focused time.

TIME FOR TASKS

To reiterate, everyone is different. Some people love schedules, some love routine, some need step-by-step actions and some need the overall bigger picture. I am pretty sure that for all of those scenarios, time blocking works. It works because in that time block, you can be as specific as you like or just give the headline and do what needs to get done.

Let me demonstrate. Time blocking is about looking at your day/week/month and saying, right, I am clear on my Big Picture (I have clarity), I know the direction I want to go in (I have the action steps), I know I want to focus on achieving that (give me the time to get it done). So you start to build your calendar AROUND the time that you want to spend working ON your business and not just IN your business.

Working in your business is providing the services, creating and sending the products, speaking to the clients. Working ON your business is putting the time aside for refining the big picture, checking that you have the resources, asking yourself if you are getting in your own way and what needs to change. Asking yourself the questions that need the CEO to answer (by the way, the CEO is you!), gaining the overarching view of the business, so that you have room and capacity for growth.

Time blocking can be as simple as:

Monday 9.00 -11.00am - Marketing strategy implementation

Wednesday 9.00-11.00am – Become up-to-date with all finances

Friday 9.00-11.00am – Content creation for newsletter, blog, vlog, TikTok, website

Once a month/quarter – CEO day to look at the Big Picture and reassess

Having done this high-level time blocking, you can then decide to get specific about the actual list of things that will get done in that time. Again, this is just an example. Do what is right for you. This can also help with where you might be better off getting something outsourced, so that your focused time is better spent on the tasks that are your strengths – what you are good at and also, what you love to do. It's your business, so love what you do with it.

I had a client who said that this couldn't work for her. I found out that was because she was trying to fit the time blocking around all her other work – the first thing to do is flip this on its head. Put the time blocking in first, and then fit everything else around it. One of those time blocks might be "Client calls" on a Tuesday afternoon – it makes it much clearer to put client calls on one or two days, so that you have the other days free for doing tasks.

Focus your time, focus your energy and get clear on what you want the outcome to be, and in what time frame.

I decided that I was going to write this book in a two week period of time, which focused my brain on getting it done. If I had told myself I had two months to write it, I would have stretched it out over that time frame.

PRIORITISING PURPOSE

Purpose is what drives your focus. Remember to reiterate to yourself why you are doing this, what it is for, what is the point in doing all the hard work, then it will be easier to prioritise it and create your focus.

The trick (if you can call it that) is to keep telling yourself how important the end result is; that this is worth your time and energy to invest in the purpose. That investing the time now will get you the outcome that you WANT, and remember that this really is about what you want to create.

If it doesn't feel important and worth prioritising, then you may need to go back and gain the clarity on the bigger picture, so that you have a clear direction to follow and then you are back on track to focus again.

SET UP YOUR ENVIRONMENT

This seems so simple, but I know that if I don't do this, then I may be working (doing), but it doesn't feel like my business-focused time. What creates your conducive work environment?

When I first thought of this and realised that it affected what I produced, it was a game-changer for me on how to get more done. I would make sure that I was sitting down to a clear desk, that I had my coffee in my favourite mug, I lit my two candles at my desk, I made sure that my office space was cool enough for me to not overheat (thank you perimenopause!), but not so cold that I needed to layer-up. You know that saying of "Dress for the job that you want, not the job you have", well, for me, that means, putting on my brightest pink top and my bright pink lippy and feeling as though I am prepared and present for the day ahead (even if it is just from the waist up – ha ha).

Consider your environment now, and how it might need to change for you to feel like the businesswoman that you are, one who wants to focus on the future growth of her business, who is driven towards her purpose and the big picture.

Be specific and then get focused!

THINGS TO DO DIFFERENTLY:

1. What is on your list of wishing, waiting and wanting? Can any of those items have your time and energy now to help you get focused on what you want?
2. What is a phrase that you can have at the ready to say to

protect your boundary of focused time? Know it, practise it, say it.

3. Create your calendar with time blocking so that you commit to focused time for your business.
4. Be specific and get focused.
5. Have your vision and mission written somewhere that you can see it, so that it prioritises your purpose.
6. Consider your working environment; is it conducive to being focused?

16

BECOMING ACCOUNTABLE

F or years I have called myself a "Clarity and Accountability Business Mentor" because I help my clients to get clear on what they want, why they want it and then, how to get it done. In the 14+ years that I have been doing this, with the hundreds of businesswomen with whom I have worked, it has been fascinating to observe the human behaviours that make a sudden, or a gradual, appearance, so that our mindset and abilities are tested.

What I have also seen is that when we are accountable to others, it makes moving forward that much easier.

BUT, this chapter is about personal accountability as much as about learning to be accountable to yourself and others.

Not only have I witnessed this in my clients, but "we teach what we need to know", I can be honest about that. I am much better at getting something done when I am accountable to someone else. As a case in point, when I was writing this book I deliberately lined up my beta-readers to be the first to read the book and give feedback so that I was accountable to a deadline. This really helps. I had a lot of people saying to me, "Why put a deadline on the writing of the book? Why put yourself under pressure?" and that bit of the equation was me being accountable to myself and getting it done.

SO WHY IS IT IMPORTANT TO BE ACCOUNTABLE TO YOURSELF?

There is a difference between taking personal responsibility and being personally accountable. I explained more about this in Chapter 12, "Why taking personal responsibility helps our mindset" but it bears repeating, so that we can be sure we are working on the right areas for our growth.

Accountability is about being able to accept the consequences of our actions and decisions. It is from that level of accountability that we are able to learn from mistakes, accept the challenges and make real changes for the future.

This is particularly important when you have your own business because it is empowering to be able to say, "This is me, I am accountable to myself, and that matters to me".

I have worked with countless people, both in the corporate sphere and through my business, who are more than happy to lay all the accountability for their decisions onto someone else because they don't want to be held accountable for the outcome themselves. In my view, this is the opposite of being a good person, let alone a good businesswoman.

What that looks like from the other side is that they are being set up to fail, they have no attachment to the outcome, other than what has been put on them, so it isn't a motivator to succeed. If you are helping others to be accountable in your business for the actions they are taking, then make sure that you are taking them on the journey of why they are working hard for you; tell them the vision for the future and how they fit into it, so that they have a sense of accountability, which feels like a driving factor for their growth, as well as yours.

Way back when I started my business, I thought that being accountable was about having a list and getting it done. It can be that, as long as you are also making sure that you have a clear idea of what you are building, the direction in which you want to go and you know where to focus your attention to get the best outcome. Then, and only then, does the feeling of accountability feel that much stronger and more of a driver towards your success.

Accountability is about ownership of your actions. "I did that, it was up to me, I accept the consequences – good or bad" ... they could be the actions that get you to a million pounds, or the actions that see you launching something to tumbleweed. Take account-ability for the good and the bad, and learn from the outcomes.

Here is why it is important to bring awareness to this. If you aren't being accountable, then who, in your mind, *is* accountable? Are you finding someone else to be accountable when things go wrong, and only accepting accountability yourself when the outcome is good?

Are you placing blame where it doesn't belong? And, if you are answering that honestly, and the answer is yes, then my Lovely, I suggest you take a good hard look at yourself and learn a different way of showing up in the world, because blaming others for your outcome isn't a very satisfying way of being a member of our global community.

DISCIPLINE AND CONSISTENCY

Sounds so serious, doesn't it? Discipline was my word of the year for 2022, because I realised that it felt more direct and powerful than accountable. During lockdown, I decided that if I wasn't going to see anyone for months or be able to go outside, then I would join an online gym to hold me accountable. As I saw it, they would be accountable for making me show up for my monthly investment, but, guess what, it wasn't their responsibility, it was mine! I had to be accountable to myself FOR myself, which is quite different from accountability in business. So I chose a different approach, and decided that I needed the constant discipline of making myself show up.

In my youth (yes, I was a youth a long time ago!), discipline meant something quite different. I was disciplined mostly for being naughty … getting the slipper at school, standing in the corner facing the wall … you know the kind of thing (please tell me I wasn't the only one who was ever-so-slightly naughty at school!), so the word discipline had a different meaning for me then than it does now. Now I consider discipline to be showing up consistently with vim-and-vigour to do the thing which leads to the outcome that I want. And the outcome that I wanted during lockdown was that my muscles didn't atrophy from complete inactivity!

The Collins English Dictionary definition of "Discipline" reads as follows: "Discipline is the quality of being able to behave and work in a controlled way which involves obeying particular rules or standards". I love that. It puts the control back in my hands, making me decide on the code of behaviours that are going to get me to my outcome, and it holds me accountable for getting it done.

CREATING YOUR MOTIVATION

I have run The Accountability Club for years and I have seen that when we choose to be accountable for the outcome towards which we are working it creates a different level of motivation. Each member brilliantly turns up, talks about their challenges and takes away their renewed commitment to what they want to get done, or create, or change, within the next two weeks. The two-week period creates the consistency in showing up; the outcome from talking helps them to work out what the challenges are, and how to over-come them, and the accountability required helps them to commit to what they want to get done. That creates the motivation to do it because they know they will be showing up again in two weeks' time. And, by golly, it works!

If we look at the "formula" here, which is an absolute formula for success if ever there was one, it is this:

challenge>solution>accountability>motivation

The thing is, in between all of the steps of the formula is the angst and the "I can't"s and the "Why me?"s.

I have been in so many year-long masterminds, programmes, coaching clubs and finding different ways of becoming accountable to what I "say" I will do, and then seeing what I actually do, and I know that it is all about the motivation behind it.

If the motivation for the outcome is strong enough, then I will listen for the solution and solve it. If the motivation isn't strong enough, then I will let my old friend procrastination pop in for a little holiday, be that for an hour, or ... oh gawd ... longer! It is up to you how long they stay. I know I make this sound so black and white, so easy peasy, and I can hear you saying, "It isn't that easy", but I implore you, question yourself the next time this happens. If you are procrastinating on something and you feel as though you need to create your own accountability, then ask yourself, "What is my motivation, and how can I make it stronger, so that I want the outcome MORE than I want to procrastinate?".

ACCOUNTABILITY IN PRACTICE

Remember that our confidence grows with preparation and practice. We are proving to ourselves that we want the outcome, so let's prepare the steps to actually become accountable ... ready?

1. What is the goal? What are you wanting to get done? Why is it important?
2. What do I need to achieve that goal? A strategy? A schedule? A plan?
3. How do I want to be kept accountable to myself? Daily goals? Key Performance Indicators (KPIs)? Weekly check-ins?
4. Create a timeline – without a deadline, you can't focus effectively, so when do you want this goal finished?

5. Get yourself an accountability buddy, or into The Accountability Club so that you don't feel as though you are doing it alone and you can find the right support.
6. Celebrate! Please celebrate each step of what you accomplish, especially if you are working your way through procrastination and angst. You need to be clear with yourself that you DID IT!

THE ABILITY TO REASSESS

I think what this all really means is, do you have the willingness to commit to getting done something that might feel hard at times?

In your reading of this book and the realisations along the way, take a good hard look at yourself, your business, your products, your services; do you love it all? If the answer to any of that is no, or things need to change, then reassess and change where you want to.

Sometimes it can feel as though we are stuck in a business which we created but which now feels like just a job that we have created for ourselves, rather than the lifestyle we wanted.

And let me be clear, this isn't all about the money. For a lot of people, it is about the time, the energy and the value that they place on themselves; these things will determine whether the money is worth it. You can have all the money in the world but not be happy, and not have a life, because you are working so much. What do you want to reassess and do differently?

I am asking this here because, if things need to change, then it is here that you can reassess those areas of your life and business. You can make clear decisions on being disciplined about changing them, and you can make sure that you want to be personally accountable for the outcome. In making those changes, you will quickly see how motivated you are and then reassess the level of accountability that you need in order to be able to get the REAL outcome that you want.

Cor blimey, that got deep ... I say it here, because I have done it. I have reassessed my life and made major changes (hello, finding my Love and getting married at 50 years old!), I have made major changes to my business and shut down profitable services because my motivation to do them and to see the outcomes was gone – and I know that I can't be accountable for something that doesn't motivate me.

Take stock, reassess where you are and what you want. When we talk about timelines and deadlines, be clear with yourself about whether they are not just reasonable, but achievable, and if they aren't, then change them, your business, your life, your rules. Reassess them, not because you are lazy, but because you know what is right for you. And make no mistake, this is all about you.

THINGS TO DO DIFFERENTLY:

1. Where can you choose to be more accountable?
2. Where do you need to add a new discipline to your life, what is a new code of behaviour that would help you?
3. What do you need to or want to reassess?

17

THE KNOWING AND THE GROWING

As we come to the end of our time together, I want to help with concrete steps for you to get out of your own way and create what you want to create.

I want to start with that pit-of-your-stomach, soul-freeing, congruent feeling when you know that what you are doing is right for you. Do you know that feeling?

THE KNOWING

When you know that something is for you, there is a whoosh and a swish of fireworks and light that starts in your stomach and bursts through your head – at least, that is what it is like for me. I have probably had it about six times in the more than 14 years that I have had my own business. It is a feeling of propulsion that sends electricity to your mind and your hands that this is right, get on and do it. It is a deep knowing that the next steps will show themselves because you are about to take the actions necessary in the direction that you know is for you.

Sometimes that sense of knowing is a feeling, or a question that gets answered, rather than a set service or product for your business. When I met my (now) husband, I knew that he was the right person for me and I had waited a long time to meet him, but I also put all the blockers in the way because my mind got in the way of my heart. But my heart was stronger, and it wouldn't let me let go of the feeling that I knew him.

Again, when I came up with the name of The Daisy Chain Group I knew it was right, it made absolute sense to me about building community, the connections with each other, the fact that a daisy chain is a cog in a machine and when that is in alignment, everything else works, that is how I help my clients, that calibration of our mind and heart that says THIS IS IT. I love the fact that daisies find their way every day to open towards the sun and shine, they are very hardy and resilient. And the fact that I have always loved daisies, and they make me happy.

The feeling of knowing comes from the alignment in yourself that this is happening at the right time in the right way for me, I KNOW this is for me.

When things are tough going, I often sit with a notebook and ask, "What do I want to be known for?". I will sit quietly and write my answer. Sometimes it is harder than others to find the words and the feeling, sometimes it takes longer to get to the crux, but if I allow myself the time to answer, there are usually about two paragraphs that, when I read them back, give me that whoosh of grounded knowledge that I am going in the right direction. OR that I need to get back to my clear messaging of what I do and how I do it. It is a re-centring, a chiropractic adjustment back to what I know to be true. True for me.

DECIDE WHAT IS TRUE FOR YOU

It is so easy to see what someone else is doing, writing or saying, and to think that you "should" be doing, writing and saying the same things. I promise you, when you start doing that, you will be losing a part of your congruency in your path of knowing.

Imagine your path of knowing is a spine, each vertebra is a piece of the puzzle that builds to your expertise, your knowledge, how you show up, what you want to be known for. When you try to believe what someone else tells you to believe, or you create a product or service because someone else makes it look so easy, or you do something because someone else told you that you would be good at it, but it doesn't fit with what you WANT to do – then it is like removing a piece of your stability, a vertebra from your spine, a chunk of your conviction – ouch!

So, decide what is true for you. Make a list of what you know for yourself. Add to it over time, check in with the list to grow your confidence.

Here is my list:

What do I know?

I know I am meant for bigger things

I know I am entertaining

I know I am driven

I know I believe in myself

I know I believe in the kindness of others

I know that everyone has the best of intentions

I know that I make a difference

I know that my events are motivating and life changing

I know that networking works when you work it

I know that, without clarity, we are pushing in a direction without knowing the outcome

I know that action breeds growth

I know that inaction feels uncomfortable and frustrating

I know that I stand for justice and fairness

I know that I champion small businesses

I know that I speak good 😋

I know that doubting myself less allows me to do more!

I have seen again and again that, when we are able to stand tall on what we know with clarity, the direction shows itself and the focus becomes an automatic response because the motivation is there to get it done. Doing this makes us stronger, more stable and allows us to build a life and a business that is purpose driven, with a sense of fulfilment. Isn't that what we all want?

THE GROWING

OK, we have been clear on what you know to be true and you are feeling the rush of YES YES YES to get it done (whatever "it" is for you), but where do you start? Well, you can start with any or all of these formulas. If you answered them all, you would honestly have most of the answers for what you want to build.

You're welcome. 😊

I have added in growth formulas because everyone looks for the magic bullet that is going to make everything happen so much faster. Newsflash: everything that means anything takes work. It doesn't have to be hard work, but it does need to be smart work. These formulas are examples of ways to get the mind thinking and a plan in place to be able to take the next action. Now that you have read the book, you will see that all of these formulas can be seen in here, and built on through reading and implementing the tips and tools from each chapter.

Ready ... Here you go!

Clarity > direction > focus - The actual steps to take are laid out in Chapters 13, 14, 15, get clear on WHAT you want, WHY you want it, and HOW to get it done!

Belief > confidence > knowing - Each of these build slowly with awareness and a change of conscious thought. Refer to Chapters 8, 9 and 17.

Know > like > trust – When people know you, they can decide if they like you, when they like you, they can build their trust in you and your business. The first thing is giving them the opportunity to get to know you. Refer to Chapter 5. You'll banish isolation and build confidence by giving time to this formula.

Clear mindset > clear strategy > clear implementation plan - first make a decision (Chapter 3), once you have a decision, you can plan for the Big Picture and how to take the actions towards it (Chapter 13), then get focused on the outcome that you WANT to create (Chapter 15).

Challenge > solution > accountability > motivation - Challenge your thinking (Chapter 3 and 4), look for what you want and don't let doubt creep in (Chapter 6), get accountable to yourself (Chapter 16), keep motivated by surrounding yourself with the best people to fuel your fire (Chapter 5).

These are all over-arching formulas, and each one needs an action plan attached so that you can achieve it. Also, be clear on what is going to work for you. Where are your strengths, and what do you need to work on? Where do you need help and support, so that you succeed?

None of this is rocket science (luckily … because I am not a rocket scientist!), but it is practical and implementable and you know where I am if you need or want help.

Pick your own adventure. And it *is* an adventure, in that it is planning the adventure, knowing where you are going, finding out how to get there and then executing the steps, seeing the outcome and celebrating what you have accomplished.

DON'T GO CHANGING

As Billy Joel said in the classic 'Just the Way You Are':

"Don't go changing, to try to please me ...

I take you just the way you are"

And this is the important bit. Work out what works for you. If you try to do what others have done and it doesn't suit your strengths, what is true for you or what you want to be known for, it isn't going to work. It is going to feel like energy draining hard work – pfft, and we don't have time for that.

We have things that we want to achieve. So just KNOW that there is an audience of potential clients out there who will take you just the way that you are ... they are waiting ... get out there and show them who you are.

THINGS TO DO DIFFERENTLY:

1. What does it feel like when you know that things are in alignment? Think of a time when you have had that *whoosh* of knowing.
2. What do you want to be known for?
3. Which formula are you going to start with? How are you going to implement it?
4. Where do you need help/support?

18

HOW TO BE MORE "DOUBT~LESS"

In my years of doubting, learning, growing, regressing, unlearning, making mistakes, facing challenges, finding people, losing people and, ultimately, writing this book, these are the things I have found:

THINGS TO DO LESS:

- Caring what others think of you
- Listening to people who aren't in your shoes
- Taking on board opinions of those who don't have their own business
- Asking for feedback from people who aren't your ideal customers/clients
- People pleasing (unless it pleases you)
- Apologising for being you
- Wasting precious energy on things that are out of your control
- Concentrating on the negative
- Procrastinating!

THINGS TO DO MORE:

- Whatever you want!
- Be who you want to be!

- Do what you want to do!
- Celebrate your accomplishments, little and big!
- Focus on what is in your control
- Concentrate on the positives
- Listen to yourself
- Work out what works for you – and then do it!
- Create what you want to create!

Everyone is always going to have an opinion, but you have to choose whether you will let their opinion cloud your judgement or whether you will decide what is right for you, and do that. You can listen to people and not implement their "helpful" suggestions – ohhh the times I have nodded my head whilst someone is ranting about what they think I "should" do because there is no point in arguing, some people just need to be heard – but not listened to – you get it!

DON'T TAKE CRITICISM FROM PEOPLE YOU WOULD NEVER GO TO FOR ADVICE

I have listened to people who have never done what I am doing and have never had to engage with an audience. I have changed my business structure, destroyed a logo, changed business services, names and ideas, and all because I listened to the wrong people who have not been where I am. I learned late to listen to people who are ahead of me in a similar business, people who have walked in my shoes and have found their path and are mentoring or helping others to do the same.

Over the years I have let my confidence be destroyed by listening to, and taking on board, the advice and opinions of people who honestly have no idea what my business is about.

I have learned to hear what my ideal clients say and then decide for myself what is important to my business growth. It distresses me when I think of all the services, products and ideas that have been squished by taking the wrong advice, or because I doubted myself or others have doubted in me – and I took on their fears. How I then regretted those decisions.

As I said at the beginning of the book, you can't regret something that you try. However, with some of these things I've just mentioned I didn't even give myself the chance to try – I let the doubt creep in and fester.

But, as I learned to do better, I did better, and that meant finding the right business and personal mentors to build me back up and say, "I have been there, I understand".

It is questioning everything for yourself and KNOWING what is true and right for you. If you aren't feeling the whoosh, don't do it.

And this is the magical piece of advice which made it a lot easier to make those decisions: *don't take criticism from someone to whom you would never go for advice.* Even if that person loves you, has known you for years and has the best of intentions, ask yourself first, would you go to them for advice and implement their advice? If the answer is no, then for the love of all things, do not listen to their well-meaning criticism of what you are doing or how you are doing it.

I told you before, part of the reason I called my previous book series "Shine On You Crazy Daisy" was because I am told that I am crazy on most things that I do, but that doesn't mean that I don't do them. I do what I want with my business; it makes it more aligned to take the personal responsibility and accountability when it goes right AND if it goes wrong, but it is always on me and my decisions, and I am good with that. It builds my character and allows Daisy Doubt~less to step in and blow away the doubts so that I feel more confident.

WHEN I DIE

When I die, I want people to say that I DID what I said I was going to do and I saw the potential in others, where they may have doubted themselves – and because of that, they DID what they said that they wanted to do too!

I want people to say, I read her book and it changed how I approached one thing and that created a ripple effect through other things.

I want people to say, that Trudy, what a character, but jeez she got her shizzle done and she helped me to grow my business too.

I want to look down from my daisy-covered cloud and whilst I am sprinkling fairy dust over everyone, they are saying, she made me laugh, and when I laughed, I felt better and because I felt better, it grew my confidence and because my confidence grew, I was able to do more, I was bolder, braver, I showed up and I shone, that started with a giggle at a networking event, or a business retreat, or an online meeting.

THAT is the power of doubting yourself less and doing more.

It isn't that we don't doubt, it is about having the tools, tips and tricks to be able to say, confidently, "I have doubted myself, but I did it anyway".

Abel Morales from *A Most Violent Year* said:

"When it feels scary to jump, that is exactly when you jump, otherwise you end up staying in the same place your whole life and that I cannot do."

CELEBRATE!

We have talked about celebrating a few times in this book. It started in Chapter 2! But as we draw to a close, please celebrate with me. Writing a book is not for the faint-hearted and I honestly didn't realise what it would take and how I would live each process again and again. The lack of self-belief when I wrote that chapter felt debilitating. The trust that I had to find in myself when I wrote the chapter about trusting yourself. The little voices of doubt that took up residence when I got to Chapter 6. So, give a little Huzzah and Hurrah to celebrate that you have finished reading what I have put my big heart into.

And, as always, I would love to celebrate you; feel free to tag me on social media when you are celebrating something; maybe something that you have implemented from this book and I will celebrate you ALL THE WAY.

And please, celebrate yourself; celebrate the past, as we talked about in Chapter 2, but also celebrate the future and all that you are planning towards your renewed direction and focus. You have got this, I KNOW it and you know it too.

THINGS TO DO DIFFERENTLY:

1. Write your list of what to do more and what to do less.
2. Whose advice do you NOT need to listen to any more?
3. Think about what you would want people to say about you when you aren't around to hear it.
4. Write a list of how you will celebrate the little and the big things

AND... Remember this:

I am enough, you are enough, this is enough.

It is in your hands. Doubt~less, DO more.

EPILOGUE

And so, Dear Readers, as the doubts have subsided and the book is written, I can reflect on the process, not just of my life, but of getting this done – and of all the ways that I have cascaded all the doubts and fears into a period of my life in getting this book out into the world.

We say it all the time in business, but, if this book helps one person, I will feel as though I have done my job. If it has helped you – please be a doubt-busting-angel and let me know through reviews on Google, Amazon etc. Those testimonials are precious words to small business owners. It is, dramatically, the wind beneath my very-large-bingo-wings.

Start a new chapter of doubting yourself less and being able to do more. Take action where you used to be stuck. I honestly didn't know that I knew this many words!

I have lived all of these processes, and I don't let doubt get in my way or stop me; it doesn't mean that I don't ever doubt myself, or that other people don't let me know all about their doubts and fears "for me", but I allow it all to wash over me … and I do it anyway!

It isn't over until the end and you decide when the end is.

Remember the daisy that opens every day towards the sun and looks for the possibilities:

~ be more Daisy.

ABOUT TRUDY SIMMONS

Trudy Simmons is a Clarity and Productivity Business Mentor for women entrepreneurs. She has a truckload of empathy and a little bit of hard-arse!

She helps you find out WHAT you want to do, WHY you want to do it, and HOW to get it DONE!

She is often described as a cross between Tigger and the Energiser Bunny, with a touch of the laughing policeman and the intense listening powers of Oprah, what a combo!

She loves to show her audience how to become more successful by getting clarity, taking action, and following through. Trudy has 20 years' experience in helping people move from being stuck and not knowing the next step, to getting their shizzle DONE by finding and harnessing their strengths and removing their weaknesses!

She knows what keeps you up at night – the thousand ideas that are germinating in your brain – and she knows how to sort them into "no go", "maybe later", and "hells yes", and get done what's really important to your success.

She's the creator and founder of:

The Champagne Collective – online mastermind days (time to work ON your business, not just in your business) – peer to peer coaching and mentoring in an encouraging environment. Bring your challenge, leave with solutions and the steps to take.

The Accountability Club – fortnightly online meetings to hold yourself accountable to what you want to get done. Asking the bigger questions to make us think bigger and do more.

1:1 Business Mentoring – you and me, getting to the nitty gritty, busting through any and all doubt and creating a business that you LOVE.

www.thedaisychaingroup.com

ABOUT THE DAISY CHAIN GROUP

Trudy Simmons started The Daisy Chain Group in 2010. It was started in order to create a safe space in which to support and encourage businesswomen and enable them to share their journeys, grow their businesses and be seen and heard in their endeavours.

Since its inception, the concept has grown to include platforms for women to find their voice and become more visible in lots of different ways. Whether it is attending online networking events, committing to co-working time together, learning from experts in masterclasses or investing in monthly business coaching to boost their clarity, direction, focus, accountability and momentum, we all need to find the space to work ON our businesses.

The Daisy Chain Group offers so many different ways to meet people, share your story, grow your audience, cultivate your confidence and be vibrantly visible, with clarity, direction and focus in your business. Please checkout the website to see what is available to support you and your business.

HAVING FUN in your business is a core value of The Daisy Chain Group. Having fun and TAKING ACTION is what builds you AND your business.

You can find The Daisy Chain Group here:

https://www.thedaisychaingroup.com

https://www.facebook.com/daisychaingroup

https://www.instagram.com/daisychaingroup/

https://www.linkedin.com/in/trudysimmons/

Shine On You Crazy Daisy Book Series: Each chapter was written by a different businesswoman, each of whom shared their journey through adversity with resilience and courage.

Shine On You Crazy Daisy – Volume 1

Shine On You Crazy Daisy – Volume 2

Shine On You Crazy Daisy – Volume 3

Shine On You Crazy Daisy – Volume 4

Shine On You Crazy Daisy – Volume 5

Shine On You Crazy Daisy – Volume 6

Available on Amazon, Apple Books and in all good bookshops.

YOU WANT MORE?

THE DOUBT~LESS WORKBOOK

Here is a QR code to get the workbook that accompanies this book to help you to doubt~less and do more! On your phone, open the camera and hold it up to this QR code, then click the link to access the workbook.

THE DOUBT~LESS PODCAST

Yes, there is a podcast! Wonderful short interviews with some very inspiring women about how they have doubted themselves, or had others doubt them, and they have done it anyway! Hearing their stories makes me feel like anything is possible – hope it is the same for you.

It is on my website and on YouTube, if you prefer to see the people who are talking.

THE DAISY CHAIN GROUP WEBSITE

Even easier to find The Daisy Chain Group website, here is the QR code to take you straight to it!

BOOKS OR PROGRAMMES I HAVE MENTIONED:

Mindset by Dr Carol Dweck

RISE Women's Empowerment Programme by

Gillian Jones-Williams from Emerge Development Consultancy

Denise Duffield-Thomas:

https://www.denisedt.com/blog/help-at-home

www.ingramcontent.com/pod-product-compliance
Lightning Source LLC
Chambersburg PA
CBHW071423210326
41597CB00020B/3625